4085 0579

What Was I Thinking?

♥

Edited by

Barbara Davilman and

Liz Dubelman

♡

What Was I Thinking?

58 Bad Boyfriend Stories

St. Martin's Press
New York

WHAT WAS I THINKING? Copyright © 2009 by Barbara Davilman and Liz Dubelman.
All rights reserved. Printed in the United States of America.
For information, address St. Martin's Press,
175 Fifth Avenue, New York, N.Y. 10010.

www.stmartins.com

Book design by Kathryn Parise

Title page illustration by Mitch O'Connell

LIBRARY OF CONGRESS CATALOGING-IN-PUBLICATION DATA

What was I thinking? : 58 bad boyfriend stories / edited by Barbara
Davilman and Liz Dubelman.—1st ed.
    p. cm.
    ISBN-13: 978-0-312-38472-2 (alk. paper)
    ISBN-10: 0-312-38472-6 (alk. paper)
    1. Man-woman relationships. 2. Women—Psychology. I. Davilman,
Barbara. II. Dubelman, Liz.

    HQ801 .W654 2009
    306.7082–dc22

                                                        2008034690

First Edition: February 2009

10 9 8 7 6 5 4 3 2 1

Copyright Acknowledgments

To my husband, Ellis,
the one man in my life who would never *show up in this book*
—Barbara

To my daughter, Grace,
whose "what was I thinking" moments are still in her future,
and my husband, Paul Slansky,
who survived my "what was I thinking" moment
—Liz

Contents

♡

Acknowledgments

♥

First, we of course want to thank all the women who submitted their work. It was an embarrassment of riches, and our only disappointment is not being able to publish all the stories we received.

This project had a very long gestation period and could not have been brought to fruition without the genius of Paca Thomas—Liz's partner in VidLit, a company dedicated to showing and telling little stories with a big impact.

We would especially like to thank Mimi Pond and Lynn Snowden Picket, who wrote pieces for us at the very beginning so we could get the VidLits off the ground. Without them, there wouldn't even be a book to write acknowledgments for.

A very special shout-out to Ms. Wendy Kamenoff, who shared her students with us—many of whom are here in the book, as is Wendy.

Our hats are off to the only man without whom this book could never have been completed: Craig Newmark, founder of craigslist .org. It was through his Web site that we were able to reach so many wonderful people.

A royal curtsey to Elizabeth Beier, our magical genie masquerading as a brilliant editor. She made all our wishes come true.

And last, but by far not least, the woman we call Downtown Patty Brown, our agent. Not only did she so completely get "us" and the project that she didn't sleep until she sold it, but she also taught us the "mwah," which we can't believe we've lived without all these years.

"Mwah" to all of you.

Introduction

♥

It all started out innocently enough: a group of women at an office trying to console a coworker the day after her boyfriend of three years gave her, for her birthday, a gift certificate for a massage.

Now, many might consider that a fine gift. But after all they'd been through, this woman wanted, and expected, and *needed,* something much more personal from him. Like an engagement ring.

We, her colleagues and friends, dutifully dragged out the well-used bag of excuses to explain away the boyfriend's insensitivity, or at least his poor taste in gifts. But she refused them all. She was done. As far as she was concerned, the relationship was over.

And then an interesting thing happened. We shifted from "rescue" to "recovery." We started sharing stories about our own previous relationships, describing that moment when *we* knew it was over. Not only did everyone have such a moment, but each of us remembered hers quite vividly—sometimes better than the relationship itself.

And so a book was born.

What Was I Thinking? is a collection of personal essays written by women describing that moment in a relationship when, no matter how much you think it should work or want it to work or need it to work, it becomes clear to you that *it's not going to work.*

It can be anything—a word used incorrectly, an insensitive comment, a glimpse of bad personal hygiene or moral weakness or breathtaking selfishness, or just an ugly sweater. In any case, the genie of disillusionment bursts out of the bottle, and there's no putting it back in.

Which is to say, this is not necessarily the moment of the actual breakup. Rather, these stories describe the instant when logic, common sense, and simple self-respect triumph over the human need to be loved—or, at least, the need to be in a relationship. The relationship may not last beyond lunch, or it may linger for weeks or even longer. But inside, you know: He's going to be an ex.

Using the Internet as our global watercooler, we put the word out through Craigslist, Facebook, and MySpace. We contacted writing programs and talked it up at cocktail parties. We found that our community was the size of the world—and that everyone had a story.

And then another interesting thing happened. The stories that started coming in were not aren't-guys-stupid? stories or are-men-necessary? stories that might conclude, however wistfully, with "No, they're not." Rather, they were stories about women looking back *at themselves*—poignantly, humorously, maybe sometimes in disbelief—to see how and why they got involved with the guy in the awful sweater in the first place.

We, as editors, as readers, and as women, want to express our extreme gratitude to, and respect for, all those whose work appears herein. Women who poured themselves a drink and then opened their diary, their heart, and even some old wounds, in order to share the stories that led to that moment when they had to ask themselves: What was I thinking?

—BARBARA DAVILMAN and LIZ DUBELMAN
Los Angeles, 2008

What Was I Thinking?

♥

A Bullwhip?

♥

Carrie Fisher

I happen to be the possessor of a very big personality. And so when I meet someone, that's where we hang out. It goes on for miles, the great outdoors, we romp around in my personality. And in my big sprawling personality, where this new someone is now, I love him. I love everything he does. I love being with him, I love sex with him, I'm charmed by him.

And what is love if not a state of enchantment? You meet someone and it puts a charm on the world. Everything looks better when you love someone and you know you're going to see him later. Everything between now and that later is so much fun to do, because you're going to get who and what you want at the end of the day, so anything's possible when that's up ahead.

Now, when the person that this happens with is someone like Paul Simon, then we're not just hanging out in my big personality. He has one, too, and they overlap in a lot of places. And that's when it's really kind of golden, when you can find someone who speaks your bizarre, bizarre dialect of a language of the smallest country in the world that hardly anyone ever visits, but they never forget having been there. Paul and I did share that, so when we got enchanted, the enchantment lasted a long time. But the problem is that, even at its best, enchantment just can't sustain.

When I date someone, I generally have about three months of a personality available and then I finally come to the end of it. I need to refuel, I short-circuit. And then whoever I'm with shows up, and a lot of the times I don't like him so much. *Now wait, I just got a little quieter and what'd you just say? You didn't read this? You've never seen that? You don't know who that is? You really think that about me?* He bothers me—not that I'm so great, but the enchantment wears off, and then the sleeping giant wakes up and says, "Fee-fi-fo-fum, I smell the blood of someone dumb."

And once that starts, it's like a case of measles, where you get just one itch one day, and then that itch spreads and spreads and spreads. And what feeds it is that he sees it happening. My face is like a Richter scale of every quake inside and outside of me, so it all shows up somehow. And if I turn the full beam on him of how much I like him and who he thinks he is, with everything that I am, if I shed that much light on him, and then that light starts diminishing, diminishing, diminishing, he notices. And I can't stop it, and the more I try to stop it the more it looks like I'm trying to stop it, and that light gets fainter and fainter and fainter until everyone's in a dark room.

I remember it specifically happening when I was going out with this guy Jesse. He was actually smart, and the enchantment was unbelievably great. I remember once we were making out at Disneyland—I was that into him that I was just publicly making out.

One night we were at my house and I was watching television, and Jesse was rubbing my back. And apparently I wasn't turning the full beam on him, because it went from zero to a thousand in a nanosecond. He said, and not nicely, "What does somebody have to do to get your attention? Wrap a bullwhip around your neck?"

What? It was like, how did we get here? I don't remember what I said in response, probably some smart-ass remark, and he put on his cowboy boots and split, drove off in his car. And I knew, I knew down to every cell of my protean body, that I would never be able to be with this guy in my life. No matter what pretzel shape I tried to bend myself into, no matter how much I tried to rationalize away what he just did, I wouldn't be able to do it. He'd just made it completely impossible for me to know him. Because some absurdities aren't funny, and you want to back away from those like they're radioactive. And I was sorry to see this cat go, because he had a nice purr.

Then he called a few minutes later, and I think I was meant to be apologetic and somehow we were going to renegotiate back into this deal. But he broke the deal. It was the one thing—well, there were several, actually—but it was one of the things you cannot do with me and survive the situation with me not thinking you're a complete asshole.

Another one of those things is to tell me, "What you're *trying* to say is . . ." I don't *try* to say anything. If anything, I try *not* to say stuff. It's effortless for me to say whatever I want to say. I don't need to go to great lengths trying to explain myself or make myself clear, or deliver to you that secret passive-aggressive message I have lurking in the back of my head that I want you to figure out after you talk to me for a while. I'll tell you. I won't *try* to tell you. "What I was *trying* to say was . . ." Oh, you know me so well. You know me better than I know myself. Wow. What else am I trying to do, now that you're so in tune to my real thoughts, real actions, real feelings? Please, give me some more insight into myself.

Once a guy shows you one of those faces that is so very different from the one he's usually walking around with, you can't pretend you didn't see it. And you know for certain that if you've seen it once, you're going to see it every time he's displeased. And people tend to get displeased, and they get disappointed, and it's your fault.

"What does someone have to do to get your attention? Wrap a bullwhip around your neck?" Yes! A bullwhip! Or maybe just, you know, like a silk rope or something, it doesn't have to be a bullwhip, the leather's so tough, but if you just get something, even like a tie, but a nice one, what would be good is if you get a nice colorful tie, wrap that around my neck, pull it *really hard,* then maybe you'll get my attention. But otherwise, you can't fuckin' have it. I'm keeping my attention to myself.

What Were They Thinking?

♥

Sara Newberry

hris and I had known each other for several years. I met him
when I was a sophomore in college and thought he was super-
cute; alas, I was involved in a serious relationship that would not end
for another year. He was smart, funny, and quirky, with dark hair and
beautiful green eyes the color of mint chocolate chip ice cream (my
favorite flavor). We ran into each other at a convenience store near
my apartment and were hot and heavy from the get-go. His hair had
thinned a little, but he was still very easy on the eyes . . . the major
difference was that when we'd met before, he'd been medicated and
his schizophrenia was under control. This time, not so much.

He moved in with me after two weeks, when he was evicted from
his apartment (he had a couch, I didn't, so win-win). I very quickly
learned that anything I said was being totally drowned out by the
voices in his head. The pinnacle (so to speak) of our group relationship occurred while we were out to dinner at a newly opened Italian
restaurant. We'd had lovely appetizers, a couple of glasses of red
wine, and were tucking into our pasta when I commented that I loved
the combination of fresh spinach and pasta. He froze, his fork halfway
between his plate and his mouth.

"You *what?*" he exclaimed, throwing down his fork.

"I . . . love . . . spinach and pasta?" I repeated, not sure what had
gone horribly wrong.

"I can't believe you just said that!" he shrieked. He threw down his napkin and stormed out of the restaurant. I wasn't sure what had happened, so I flagged down our waiter, paid the check (did I mention Chris didn't have a job?), and headed out to the parking lot, where he waited next to my car (um, yeah, I know).

"What is your problem?" I asked, throwing the door open and getting in. He sat down in the passenger seat.

"I can't believe you just admitted that you've been cheating on me this whole time!"

I was stunned, to say the least. We dated for several more months before he moved out, after he got a job wearing a sandwich board for a bead store. I have since raised my standards. And I still love spinach and pasta.

Speaking My Language

♥

Courtenay Hameister

I've thought about it a lot, and I'm pretty sure the man I think was the love of my life . . . probably wasn't the love of my life.

See, he loved me and I loved him, but I think the me he loved wasn't really me, and the him I loved was a him I'd made up in my head a long time ago, and then dressed him in a love-of-my-life suit.

The me he loved was a person I'm sure everyone else in my life wouldn't recognize. I was like a gratitude machine, always trying to make up for his being such a generous humanitarian, what with the whole "loving me" thing and all. Every day, I'd be glad to add something of his to my to-do list. "Honey? Is there anything you need? Pick up your dry cleaning? Clean out your garage? A lifetime supply of earth-shattering blow jobs? Because, seriously, I don't have anything else to do right now." Who wouldn't fall in love with that person? It was like I was Julia Roberts in *Pretty Woman*. Except he wasn't paying me. And I wasn't in thigh-high, patent-leather boots. Well, at least not *all* the time.

The him that I loved—well, the real . . . let's just call him Judgy McSex-a-lot—was a series of contradictions. He was a marathon runner, but he smoked. He was supportive, but judgmental. He seemed emotionally distant most of the time, but at other times his sweetness would put me into a blissful sugar coma. I awoke one morning to find him watching me sleep. He smiled and just said one word: "Pretty." How does a person not get sucked in by that?

In possibly the only instance in my life where I might have been deemed a Pollyanna, I chose to concentrate on only the good things. So what if he smokes—he's great in the sack! So what if he's quiet—he's so smart! So what if he's probably an alcoholic, and always gives me shit about not being able to fix my relationship with food—he's got good hair! I wouldn't say that I was looking at him through rose-colored glasses—in fact, it was just the opposite. I chose to take my glasses off to look at him—that way the looming clouds of our uncomfortable dinner conversations, his utter lack of a sense of humor, and his narcissism, just looked like pretty fuzzy marshmallows, floating happily above our heads. It may have been the one time I was finally able to put my astigmatism to good use.

I was still squinting happily through our days together when he dumped me after a year. It was an ugly breakup that left me emotionally hobbled for upward of another year.

Immediately after the breakup, I got reacquainted with all my old friends. Mrs. Fields was as much of a hoot as she'd ever been. The Entenmanns were a delight to have over for breakfast, or lunch, or any one of the three dinners a person might have in one night. And Oscar and, really, the entire Mayer clan, were nothing if not staunchly supportive.

I started gaining weight, and fast. And as soon as I could see it on me, I knew I could never see Judgy again. Not that I wanted to—after the dumping, I avoided seeing him like plague. Well, not like the plague, because I don't do a lot to avoid the plague these days. I avoided seeing him like AIDS. I steered clear of his neighborhood, all of our shared friends, and anything having to do with his business, environmental geology. This was the hardest part, it turned out, because you can't swing a dead piece of tofu in Portland, Oregon, without whacking an environmental geologist in his holier-than-thou head.

But thankfully we never crossed paths in those few months, since the last thing I wanted was for him to see me. Almost a year post-breakup, I'd gained fifteen pounds. Glasses still off, I continued inexplicably to be devastated by the loss of him. Right around then, the radio show I worked on started getting some real attention from the press. A local magazine decided to run a feature article on the show. I was mortified. I told my therapist, and she was perplexed by my strange reaction to this great news.

"I've been in the paper before," I told her, "and I felt the same way. I just keep picturing the same scenario. He's at work, reading the paper with his coworkers at lunch. They come upon the story and the picture of me and he says, 'Wow. Look how fat she got. I guess I dodged a bullet there, huh?' And then, in my head, he laughs in this cruel, frat-boy way even though he was never in a frat."

There were lots of times I could see my therapist editing herself . . . sitting in her warmly appointed office, surrounded by colors and fabrics designed to make me feel comforted and accepted, and trying everything in her power not to fly out of her comfy leather chair and throttle me until I returned from my yearlong vacation in Crazytown. (Which, by the way, is only a quick train ride away from Funkytown, which I've heard is much more fun.) She managed to hold herself back, but I could see her frustration as she rubbed her forehead.

"How often do you imagine this scenario?" she asked.

"Every time my picture's in the paper. Or on our Web site. And he always says the same thing: 'I guess I dodged a bullet, there, huh?'"

"Did you ever hear him use that phrase in real life?" she asked.

"Never," I replied.

"So what does that tell you about the likelihood of that scenario happening?"

"Um. It makes it less likely?"

"Exactly."

I didn't buy it. She told me to offset that image with one that most noncrazy people have when something swell like getting good press happens to them—one of smiling, supportive strangers and friends reading it and being happy for me. What a crock of shit. No one smiles while they read the paper.

Six months later, I was better. Fifteen more pounds heavier, but better. I could see him a bit more clearly, but his foibles were still a bit fuzzy. Looking back on our relationship, it was a lot like having mental TiVo, watching the good parts over and over again while fast-forwarding through the bad. I wondered if I'd ever get over him and so did every person in my life. They'd gotten over him immediately. What the hell was wrong with *me*?

That spring I took a weekend trip to New Mexico for a film festival with a group of friends who I'd worked with on a short film. We were all set to go to one of the illuminating seminars when someone mentioned margaritas. It doesn't take long to weigh the respective merits of those two words against each other. Seminar. Margarita. You try it and see where you net out. I'll wait.

We drove around the outskirts of Albuquerque until we found a perfect hole-in-the-wall spot to drown our boredom. As we walked to the restaurant, we noticed that there was a psychic across the street. After a few margaritas, going to see her was deemed a necessity and not going to see her was, apparently, for pussies. So I knocked on her door.

I walked into an environment not unlike my therapist's. A thirty-something woman with much better hair than mine sat at a rustic wood table surrounded by tasteful southwestern art. Dressed in a khaki skirt and a sweater set straight out of J.Crew, she looked surprisingly not nuts.

I sat down and she asked me what I wanted to know. I desperately wanted to ask her the standard "When will I find love again?" question, but I didn't want to seem . . . well, desperate. "Whatever you want to tell me," I replied. She whipped out the tarot cards and smiled.

"Well, let's just see what happens."

She laid out the cards, periodically making "hmph" noises. When she was finished, she looked concerned.

"Wow," she said. "I see a very charismatic man here who's really informing your life."

I couldn't think of who she meant.

"He's charming, but . . . he's got a lot of rules."

Hmm . . . nope. No one comes to mind.

"It looks like you got involved with him thinking that it would be good for your self-esteem, but now you just feel small."

That's . . . okay, that's weird, but that describes about half the relationships I know.

"He tried to make you think you had a problem, that you were a mess . . . but he was the one with the disease."

She took one last look at the cards and then really looked at me, making sure she had my full attention.

"Ya know, you dodged a bullet with that one, right? You would've lost yourself completely."

My breath caught in my throat, and suddenly I was totally sober. At the same second, I was slapped with two harsh realities: one, she was absolutely right and I'd wasted almost two years mourning a relationship that never existed, and two, psychics were totally real.

I walked out of her storefront realizing that this stranger had just said the exact same thing that every person in my life had been telling me all along. It's just that she spoke my language.

Our short film took top honors at the film festival, and when we got back to town, our pictures were in the paper.

I was proud and happy.

Shaking

♡

Francesca Lia Block

I'm at an outdoor concert, dancing near you, but you aren't really with me. Your eyes are distant. You shake your hips gracefully, moving sinuously from your pelvis. I remember the first time we danced together. We hadn't made love yet. The tension was so great you wouldn't let my body rub up against yours. But also you never looked away.

The woman approaches; predatory, focused. She is about my age and body type with straight dark hair and tight white jeans, a white camisole, something I would wear, though tonight I'm in a pink and gold lace top and a silky skirt.

I have been advised, when another woman tries to hit on your man, gently touch his arm, remind him you are there. I want to run away, but instead I make myself put my hand gently on your back. You ignore my touch. It's as if you can't feel me at all. You keep dancing and the woman keeps shaking her ass in your face. I walk away.

Later I return and she is still dancing near you, chatting, asking you questions. I try again to let you both know I am here, with you, your girlfriend. I thought I was your girlfriend. We have been making love once a week, though only that, and I'm always the one who calls, for a year. You have told me you love me and that you have never felt so close to anyone. I watch your child for you; you have held my children's hands, gone to their recitals, bought them things. You have taken my photograph to show me myself.

Now you ignore me again. I'm not the girl in the photo, the center of your attention, the picture in your eye. I'm invisible, even in pink and gold lace, even dancing.

I say, "I'm going to go now."

You look at me coldly and say, "Okay. See you later." You do not touch me.

I walk away and stop. The Brazilian music is like flames leaping around me. There is a singed smell, but I realize it is coming from inside my body. My girlfriends hold me while I shake and sob. No one can hear me because the music is so loud. It is both my protection and my attacker.

I am crying too hard, but it isn't just because of what just happened. There are other things happening. Between us. Not about us. Or not directly. Like the fact that I've already given notice and the loan might not go through on the little yellow cottage I'm trying to purchase, the little house with the roses in front and the mermaid bathroom and the pond. I'm worried that I may not have a place to live. You're worried that I'm going to ask you to move in with me. But that moment when you won't acknowledge me holds in it all the loss of what we have had, a hundred love poems sent to you, unanswered. My sacred dances for your pleasure, but not as your partner. The rooms lit with candles where you never came while looking at my face, always from behind. The way you never introduced me to your friends and pretended to everyone that we were not moaning and shaking with love the night before.

In a hospital your wife is pregnant with another man's baby. She is young and beautiful and left you suddenly. You have kept me a secret from her, too. When we first were together you called her your ex, but when I got divorced you said, "Congratulations. I still haven't done that." When I asked you why, you explained it was financial. She wants the divorce, but she told you that she also wants her new son to have your last name along with his father's.

The gorgeous Brazilian singer with her long braids and bright colors has a voice like ripe, sun-warmed fruit and the drums are in my heart, but none of it is beautiful anymore. Nothing is over yet, not for a month or so, but I know I will never see that country where I dreamed we might go to see your family and dance together in the streets.

Not even here, in this city where I was born and will die, not even here can we dance together.

After I calm down I start to leave with my friends and I see you. I go over and hug you, trying to be loving, trying to be mature. You hold me at arm's distance after a moment. "I thought you left," you say, so cool.

We make love the next night, but I don't say a thing about what happened. I wait four days, talk to my therapist. Then I call and ask, "If we are out together and someone hits on either of us, will you put your arm around me to let them know we are together?" You say, "I don't have a problem with that." But when I bring up the woman at the concert you say, "I know she was hitting on me. I know you were upset. I didn't want to deal with it. Besides, after you left, she told me, 'I'm going to go meet my boyfriend now.'"

This is said to make me feel relieved—she had a boyfriend and wouldn't have really taken it further with you. But it makes me feel worse. How did it get to the point that she even told you about her boyfriend, that she even needed to let you know she wouldn't be going home with you? It really shouldn't have been a question. I was with you. Or was I? We didn't come together.

In bed or out, we rarely do.

But three weeks later we are in the gurgling, twinkling backyard of my little yellow dream house where we made love once on the lawn and talked about making love in every room and you are telling me you need space, you like your independence, you don't want a girlfriend. We had something great, but it's not working now.

I am crying and sobbing on the steps in my garden. I say, "Tell me something, please, give me something." You only once told me I was beautiful, when I begged you. You said, "You really need validation, don't you?" Now you say, "You're beautiful. You're an amazing person. People love you. It's breaking my heart to see you like this. Maybe I'm stupid."

For that moment, I feel the love you had for me. Then it's gone. You are talking about us in the past tense again.

I know you want to leave. I put my hand on your leg. I say, "Go now. You can go." And you slip back through my new house, out my front door, and into your car, quick and quiet as a black cat. I wonder if you can still hear my sobs from the street.

It's just like a dance, isn't it? This dancing toward each other, coming together shaking with life and desire, this union, this farewell, this standing alone in the darkness, gazing out over the crowd to the brightly lit stage where the beautiful woman sings our dreams and then they are gone, she's gone, the night is completely silent. And still.

My Date with Homer

♥

Sarah Downie

I was dating this man, a very respectable executive. Divorced, with three lovely children, several houses, athletic build, and a nice (if a little bland) personality. Things were going okay, except, well, there was not much of a click. In any event, we had gone on several dates and appeared to enjoy each other's company well enough.

One evening we were out at a nice, if somewhat trendy, restaurant. I got a little tipsy because, frankly, he was boring me and I was nervous. (Does he want to have sex with me? Do I want to have sex with him?) The dinner was almost over and we were enjoying some dessert and we started talking about our families. He mentioned that he got asked a lot about the series *Big Love* because of his family history. Not knowing much about his family history, I asked, with some trepidation, "What do you mean?" He said, "Oh, I thought I had told you" (which is a dead giveaway that he was dating other women at the time and had told one of them, but I digress). He said, "My grandfather was a polygamist. He had several wives."

Now, notwithstanding that my date himself appeared for all intents and purposes *not* to be a polygamist, and several times told me how bad polygamy was, I could not get the image of his polygamist grandfather out of my head. In my head his grandfather morphed, not into Joseph Smith, but into Jebediah Springfield of *Simpsons* fame (who may or may not have been a polygamist—the details are murky), and my date morphed into Homer Simpson. I thought to myself, There's no way I'm dating Homer Simpson. And that was it. I was through with the indirect spawn of polygamy. I hope that he is now dating someone who doesn't watch as many cartoons.

Opera

♡

Betty Goldstein

I've always loved the opera, since I was a little girl. Every Saturday night, my family sat around the radio and listened to *My Music,* BBC's version of *Name That Tune* for opera trivia geeks. I'm still pretty good at it.

My parents never took us to the opera, yet we owned numerous operatic and symphonic recordings on 33⅓ vinyl. Mom sang the lullaby from *Hänsel und Gretel* when she tucked us in, and often hummed haunting melodies in her lovely contralto voice.

In the early 1970s, I moved to Venice, Italy, because I married a Venetian. My husband did not appreciate the opera. He never took me to Teatro La Fenice, the elegant opera house where *La Traviata* and *Rigoletto* premiered. My hubby had other redeeming qualities, such as a libido so formidable I still blush, and sweet parents who treated me with kindness.

One day while chopping vegetables for *una zuppa minestrone* in my Italian *cucina,* RAI Due, channel 2 on the Italian radio, was playing "Una Furtiva Lagrima" ("A Furtive Tear") from Donizetti's opera *L'Elisir d'Amore.* I froze with cleaver in hand, sticky with garlic and onion.

As the character Nemorino prayed for his own swift death should the love potion fail to bewitch Adina, the woman of his dreams, it was I who was under the spell of the magical elixir. I swooned in complete surrender to the ardent young tenor with the voice of silver. The possibility of impending consummation of Nemorino's aching love made me tremble and weep. Dear *God,* may this awesome aria never end.

At that precise moment, my Venetian husband entered the room and changed the station so he could listen to the soccer game.

I did what any opera buff would do. I got a divorce.

Junk in the Trunk

♥

Amy Wruble

I knew it wasn't going to work out with Phil about halfway through our first date. Bobby, eager to pair off his single friends, had invited both of us to dinner in SoHo without much thought to our compatibility. Phil was short and slender, with small, pointy, feminine features, like a ferret in drag. I wasn't going to let his looks thwart the possibility of a romantic connection. It was January and I'd just made a resolution to be less superficial in the New Year. All my life, I'd been a single white female seeking an intellectual male supermodel. (Have you met my husband, Dr. Matthew McConaughey, M.D., Ph.D.?) This was a lot like trying to date the Loch Ness Monster. I was ready to admit that the species was just a myth.

Along the way, I'd dated a string of sexy scarecrows, still waiting for the Wizard to grant them a brain. There was the chiseled musician who can best be described as half-lingual. His rock band should have been called Malapropism. He once ordered the "cheese fondude." There are only so many times you can shut somebody up with kisses, especially in a restaurant. Then came the adorable pot dealer whose remedial math skills almost got him beat up when he shortchanged a client by confusing a pound with two and a half ounces. A high school dropout, he lacked book knowledge. (His Achilles' heel was not knowing where his Achilles' heel was.) Dating these cute dopes had left me with nothing but pretty photographs, huge credit card bills, and an STD scare. But Phil, my blind date, came from a nice family, went to a good school, and had a big-boy job in finance, so I was going to look right past that girlish rodent face and into his beautiful (I hoped) soul.

The restaurant was small and unpopular. We ordered drinks and appetizers and got to know each other a bit, with Bobby playing host. "Phil, you and Amy have something in common. You're both from Connecticut." Me: "Really, what part?" Him: "Westport." Me: "I'm from Stamford." Him: "Oh." So maybe we didn't have a cosmic connection, but I was still cheerily optimistic that Phil had something charming or special about him waiting to be revealed.

At some point I got up to pee, locating the tiny, drafty bathroom across the way. There I was, jeans down around my ankles in the stall, when I heard voices, loud and clear, like they were next to me. It was Bobby asking Phil, "So what do you think of Amy?" Through some trick of the acoustics, the sound of their conversation had traveled up into the ceiling rafters and down into the bathroom as easily as water through pipes. "She's a nice girl . . . ," Phil began. I stopped peeing so I could hear even better. This was a rare opportunity, the realization of that fantasy where I'm invisible and can hear what everyone's saying about me. "But you know," Phil continued, "she's got a lot of junk in the trunk." I was stunned. If this had been a reality show, one of those record-scratching sound effects would have really captured the moment.

For anyone not familiar, "junk in the trunk" is a derogatory reference to the size of a woman's behind. So let me set the record straight about my ass, before it sues me for slander. My ass is one of the least objectionable parts of my body. It's round, it's firm, it has pizzazz. And ever since J. Lo and Beyoncé embraced bootyliciousness, it's even trendy. If my ass had a job, it would be entertaining the troops in the U.S.O. If my ass had a name, it would be Lola. My trunk has spunk. Now, had Phil directed his critique elsewhere—say, my training bra boobs or the premenstrual volcano on my chin, I might have stayed locked in the bathroom all night, tearful and humiliated. But his critique wasn't so much hurtful as ironic. Here I was, renouncing my superficiality, pledging to embrace inner beauty, and the ferret face thinks I've got a big butt.

I returned to the table, wondering how and when to expose my secret knowledge. (You didn't think I was going to let this one slide, did you?) The opportunity presented itself when the waitress asked if we wanted dessert. Phil turned to me: "Do you want to split something?" I paused, looked deeply into his eyes, and told him, "I don't think so. I want to be careful not to put too much . . . junk in my trunk." Something flickered in his face. Phil didn't acknowledge my comment, but I knew he'd heard me. I wondered if he thought I was psychic, or just had supersonic ears. I wondered if he felt guilty or was simply relieved to know our brief relationship had come to an end. (Insert record-scratching sound here again.)

In that moment I reevaluated my New Year's resolution. Maybe it's okay to be a little superficial. When I'm genuinely attracted to a man, I'm flirtier, warmer, and a better date, making him more likely to appreciate my total package instead of appraising my parts. Maybe I just need to balance physical attraction with some deeper qualities like kindness and being good at Scrabble. Months later, I heard Phil turned gay. Okay, that's not strictly true, but it's what I like to tell myself, and Lola.

Star Light, Star Bright

Claudia Handler

I had been told I could never have a baby, and so, when I got pregnant—after ten years of not using birth control—it was more than a big surprise. It was earth-shattering. It was like finding out the sweet old lady you smiled at in the supermarket had died, and left her house on the cliff overlooking the ocean to you.

When it happened, I had been living, for three years, with a guy I had known since I was eleven. Jake was quick-witted and fun, a guitarist and songwriter, and together we wrote and recorded songs, performed them with our band, and released a few CDs. He taught me the joys and frustrations of creative collaboration, a process I found both supremely difficult and wildly exciting.

In addition to his sense of humor and talents as a musician, Jake was very involved with food and wine. He loved to entertain, and would frequently spend hours preparing meals. He was one of those people who would start thinking about what he would make for dinner, and which wine he would serve, right after he woke up.

Our daughter, when she arrived, was a two-hundred-watter, thrilled to be alive, and resistant to all things she perceived as impinging on her ability to live life to the fullest. Early on, therefore, sleep became her enemy. And since Jake was always busy making dinner, the task of putting Lily to bed fell to me.

One night we had company, which made her particularly uninterested in seeing her day come to a close. But when her bedtime came, I excused myself, carried her to her room, put her in her crib, and began to sing a lullaby, which was pretty much what I did every night.

"Look, little baby, there's a star in the sky. Oh wait, little baby, there's another star in the sky. That makes two stars in the sky." I sang as gently as I could, in a voice intended to soothe and to lull her, soft, like wind through wheat. "Look, little baby, there are two stars in the sky. Oh wait, little baby, there's another star in the sky. That makes three stars in the sky. Look, little baby, there are three stars in the sky. Oh wait, little baby . . ."

It was one of those counting songs that could go on forever, and was intended, basically, to bore the child to sleep.

I sang and rubbed her back until there were ten stars in the sky. Until there were thirty stars. Until there were fifty. When my hand fell asleep, I switched hands, and continued to sing until there were ninety stars in the sky. At last, she was beginning to settle. After about two hundred stars, I finally hit pay dirt. She was out.

I leaned my head back and sat there as quietly as I could, afraid to move. I had been in her room for more than an hour, and decided I might as well play it safe by staying in there for a few more minutes, in case opening the door would rouse her, and force me to start the process all over again.

As I waited, I listened to the talk coming from the dinner table. I heard one of our friends, the drummer in our band, ask Jake how his life had changed since he had become a father. And that's when I heard it, that's when I heard this delightfully funny, talented man, whom I loved, who was my creative partner, who put delicious food on my plate every night, and, above all else, had managed to get me pregnant, so that a dream I had to let go of became a luscious reality, reply, "Well, actually, my life really hasn't changed that much. But Claudia's sure has."

I guess it's the same for everybody. When you hear the truth, you know it. I held my breath. Point taken. Ax blow delivered, deeply, with precision.

Jake was right about one thing. My life sure had changed. It was utterly unlike the life I led before I became a mother. What I had not realized, however, was that he felt his life had not changed much. I wondered how that was possible. How could becoming a father not change your life?

As that realization settled on me, like dust from a nuclear explosion, I also realized that this was the way it was going to be. He would keep on thinking about the food he would cook, the wine he would drink, and whom he would invite for dinner, and continue to lead a basically unchanged existence, while I grew more and more involved with our kid. And at that moment, with the force of a missile tearing through metal, I mourned the food that would never be eaten, the songs that would never be written, and the lives that would never be shared, and realized, as fully as I had ever realized anything, that this was a situation that was never going to work.

It wasn't long after that night that I no longer ate meals that took hours to prepare. I no longer had wine with dinner. On the contrary, dinner became a rather simple affair. I might have a bowl of egg noodles, or tuna, perhaps, dumped straight from the can onto a plate, with a tall glass of chocolate milk on the side, while the baby sat propped up and twinkling at me, like a sky, filled to the brim with stars, right there in the middle of the table.

The Yogi

♡

Kerri Cesene

He stood in a stream of sunlight, perfect posture, arms out in a perfect T, and each perfect sinewy muscle glowing on his tall skinny frame. I thought he looked like Jesus. After class I told him so.

Later we were lying naked on his futon in his one-room apartment on the beach. I couldn't believe it. He was so beautiful! And he was a yoga teacher, so he must be very, very deep. This was going to be special. This was going to be real. He pulled me on top. I smiled and leaned down to kiss his sacred lips. I closed my eyes. Then I felt . . . his hand . . . on my . . . shoulder . . . which he gently rolled back . . . and I thought, Ohmygod, is he correcting my posture? During sex?!?

Since then I've been amazed to discover how many douche bags become yoga teachers.

Revenge Baby

♡

Rhonda Talbot

I gazed into his deep-set emerald eyes, exchanging wedding vows in a small, empty Vegas chapel called something like "Any Pregnant Whore Can Get Married Here." I knew once the baby was born, Emerald would be packing his bags. I knew he was cheating on me. I knew he was standing before me out of some leftover Lutheran guilt. I knew he didn't like my tits. I knew he didn't like my blond hair because he constantly told me his preference was for darker, more "exotic" women. I knew I would be a single parent. I knew he would be a deadbeat father. I knew this moment of obligation was nothing more than that. But I also knew there was no way I was turning back. I was getting that ring on my swollen finger and to hell with all that other stuff.

For some reason, during this ceremony, the midget passing for a pastor had accidentally put in the *Star Wars* theme tape. That cost us an extra fifty bucks. For another fifty I bought myself a bouquet of wilting white roses. I also had paid for the rings, all of the gas as we sped down the 10 Freeway and signed a prenup he scribbled together while chain-smoking. (To his credit, he did blow the smoke out the window.) I would also end up paying for our cheap hotel room. But in all fairness, Emerald paid for our wedding night all-you-can-eat buffet. He also sprang for the marital license, though I had to stand in a long line in the Vegas courthouse. Alone. Emerald gets antsy in any place that smells like a correctional facility. But I wasn't really alone because there were eight or so other pregnant girls, all of us pretending like this was normal.

So there we stood, my soon-to-be husband and I, uttering things like "to have and to hold." These words fell from my mouth like dirty nickels, all tinny and out of place. To have and to hold what exactly? Six months pregnant, all I was thinking about was holding the baby. Alone. Meanwhile, Emerald was being utterly sincere. He made me believe he would stand by me no matter what, for the rest of our lives, until death do us part! He whipped out some vows he had written somewhere between the hotel room and the chapel. I was so surprised with his recitation of gratitude and respect for me, my eyes became cartoon pinwheels. He was so convincing and, in that spellbound moment, I chose not to remember he was an actor. I vowed in my early single years to never even date actors, so the fact that I was with child and marrying one seemed like a page out of someone else's life. What was I thinking indeed!

Cut to: a few months prior. Location: Carmel. Interior: costly hotel. Setting: an enormous balcony overlooking the foamy Pacific. The reason: we had dated for a year (during which we wrote a screenplay), broke up, sold said screenplay, and now had to rewrite the damn thing. We both decided we may as well do it in Carmel, particularly since someone else was picking up the tab and since we were there, why waste the atmosphere? We might as well have sex. So, this was the morning after what I thought was very soulful and connected sex. Maybe we had been too hasty in the breakup, after all.

Emerald sat across from me, smiling, holding my gaze in the way only certain actors can do that somehow pins you to your chair and makes the rest of the universe vanish, including that vast ocean. I was experiencing a moment of what could have been bliss. Then he spoke.

"Um. I just want you to know, our sex last night. Wow." Here it was. Emerald was finally going to tell me he had that revelation. The one I had hoped he would reach. The one where he realized I was, in fact, the one. He could look past my small tits, my blond hair, my lack of sex appeal, the fact that I didn't own fuck-me boots, or that I was never institutionalized for Frances Farmer–like behavior. He was in love with me. I was doing a fast mental Rolodex of our friends. Who would come to the wedding? Where would we have the ceremony? His hometown of Cowpoke, Utah? The coast of Los Angeles? Where will we live? Certainly not his shithole apartment. He was on a network series now. We could get one of those nice duplexes on Sycamore. We were about to start our life. I suddenly felt a little shy. I tried to keep the stare going.

"I know. Right? I felt that, too."

Pinwheel eyes.

"Well, the thing is, during our sex, all I kept thinking about was another woman. I really can't explain why. The entire time I was inside of you, I just was thinking of her almost like she was there, right there with us."

My face must have gone pale because he kept saying, "Are you okay? Is it the eggs?" I don't remember dropping my fork. I do remember feeling nauseous.

He reached for my hand, which was no longer attached to my arm.

"I have to be completely honest," he went on. "Or this will never work out. I feel like I can trust you enough to say these things. It's not in any way to hurt you. I never want to hurt you."

I pulled my plastic hand back and put it on my lap, hoping if I tucked it under my thigh, it might feel real again.

"Of course. Why would I be hurt? That's totally fine. Your honesty is all that matters, right? So, who is it? I mean, since you're being completely honest. I'm just curious now. Who were you thinking about?"

He paused. Slurped his coffee.

"Muriel Williams."

"The come-and-get-your-miracles girl?" I shouted. "Why?"

"Well. We met at one of her seminars and totally connected. I can't get her out of my head. I just needed you to know that."

"Okay. Well. Thanks for telling me."

I would have to endure another week in this beautiful hotel with this idiot. I didn't have any more sex with him. Now it was strictly work. But he was on the phone seven hours a day with Muriel. No doubt getting all sorts of miracles bestowed upon him.

I paced around the lush hotel room that we weren't paying for, spewing information.

"You can't just get miracles, dumb ass! You have to earn them! That is so fucking lame. Isn't she a fag hag? She has zero fashion sense. She looks anorexic! Her tits are smaller than mine! Her hair is orange!" I was relentless.

We returned home, handed in what was probably the worst piece of writing to ever arrive in Hollywood, and I tried to forget him and the entire ordeal. But as messed up as I was in my twenties, I couldn't get the guy out of my head. What did Muriel have that I didn't? She parroted platitudes from a book she didn't even write! I knew for certain she was not mentally ill, or a prostitute, or anything Emerald held in high esteem. I started to drive by her house, peek in her windows, call and hang up when she answered. This girl was a bore! I didn't have the patience to actually sit through one of her seminars. I also followed Emerald. I broke into his apartment, looked through his hundreds of egocentric journals for clues. Why her? Why not me? I listened to his messages.

"Your penis reminds me of a long smooth bolt of expensive material." What? I stood in his apartment, contemplating the hundreds of fleas jumping out of the rug. She did the sex talk thing. Was that it? I kept reading the journals. I couldn't tell if the stuff was real or imagined, but when I got to the section where he described one of his sexual conquests as having a bear trap in her vagina I had to stop. That didn't bother me so much as I was never mentioned. Not even one time. In all those entries! At least he didn't see me like the vagina trap, but I guess he didn't see me at all.

As I left his apartment, I took a pint of Häagen-Dazs from the freezer and threw it at his fleabag cat whose name, of course, was Pussy. I missed, but the carton exploded against the kitchen wall. My friends kept telling me to forget the guy. Have sex with someone else. Blast the guy right out of your mind. Torpedo sex. Usually does the trick. I didn't want to do this, but I was still so obsessed with him I was willing to give it a try. Being the extreme person I am, I set up three dates for one day. I had morning sex with the apartment complex surfer, afternoon sex with this guy I had met once at a rifle range, and nighttime sex on a proper date with a film executive who had passed on one of my screenplays: "Fresh writing, but there was no second act." After I had reached all the satisfaction I knew I was going to receive from the film exec, I asked him to leave. He was not happy as his needs had not been met. I yawned and explained the first act was so uneventful I simply couldn't continue.

I woke up the next morning, feeling hopeful. I looked out my small, cheap apartment window into the neighbor's sundeck and watched as he yelled at his Scottish terrier for peeing on the carpet. What a meanie. I jumped up to yell at him, when I realized I wasn't thinking about Emerald! It had worked. So overjoyed, I danced over to a counter pretending to be my kitchen and fired up the coffeepot. Coffee. Emerald. No. It didn't work. All I could see was his face. And hers! What were they doing? What were they talking about? Why is she even interesting! I boiled water. I had to know, so I called him.

"It's me. My neighbor is yelling at his dog again. What should I do?"

"Look, R, I know this is hard for you. But we are living together now."

"*Eewwww!*"

He sighed into the phone.

"What we had was wonderful, but I've moved on and you need to as well. And please stop calling and hanging up. We know it's you." Click.

I dropped to my knees. So humiliated I wanted to vomit, but then I actually did vomit. Washing my face, I noticed my breasts had grown one full cup size in a week. Plus they were tender. And there it was. The answer to it all. My pregnancy surprise sent me into a state of complete ecstasy. I ran out to my ledge masquerading as a balcony and laughed. A happy laugh. I suddenly saw into my future and it was clear. I am having the baby no matter what. My little Carmel creation. Fuck Emerald and fuck Muriel. This baby will not only keep me preoccupied and my mind off of Emerald, but it will totally mess up anything he's got going on with miracle girl. A sweeter revenge I could not imagine.

So that is how we ended up in Vegas.

"I'm having the baby. You can do whatever you want. I just thought you should know because I believe in being totally honest. I'm also dating. And surprisingly a lot of guys find it sexy. My tits are huge. Lots of guys it turns out want to be dads. And love the idea that this is like a sperm donor situation. Who knew?"

Emerald couldn't cope with this. So he broke it off with the miracle worker and moved into my apartment. I bought a size fourteen dress for the wedding and we asked some bum on Vegas Boulevard to be our witness (it was cheaper than the ones the chapel provided).

I learned that you can stay in a relationship long after the "what the hell was I thinking" moment, and even force it into a marriage. But in the end, the thing wilts faster than Vegas chapel roses. That baby is now an outstanding young man and to date, the best contribution I have made to this world. Emerald is still chasing miracles, but I never went down the "ignore the red flags" path again. Perhaps it was growing up, perhaps motherhood. But from the day Emerald walked out of my life, as I held our newborn, it was as though I was reborn from a pathetic needy girl into a woman of substance.

The Crying Game

♡

Laurie Winer

I know a woman who said she woke up one morning and realized she had to get out of her ten-year marriage. I believe her, but I think her big epiphany was preceded by a hundred smaller ones, each one of those cushioned by a whole lot of suppression. New relationships, on the other hand, can really be over in a flash—and in that flash something is made clear that can never be muddy again. No agonizing is necessary. The future, she be here.

Transitional relationships, on the other hand, lend themselves to the flash-ending technique. Aside from the obvious definition, I would say a transitional relationship is one that you get into to straighten out the imbalance of the last relationship. So the playing field on which you start the game is uneven. One day, someone hits a foul ball, it lands inbounds, and the inherent wrongness of the whole venture is laid bare.

As for me, I had been with a boyfriend for nine years, sort of a first marriage without the paperwork. He was wonderful and comfortable. But, as vaguely bored young women do every day, I had to blow it all up to see what else might be out there in the big, wide world. I rushed heedlessly but happily into the arms of an exciting and undependable individual whose motives and desires I misread every step of the way until I wound up flat on my ass, emotionally speaking.

After a nasty bruising, you look for kindness at all costs. I remember the moment I fell for Transition Boy; it was as trivial as the ending.

I met Transition Boy at my friend's apartment. A bunch of us were there one night, watching TV. When the bell rang, he went to answer the door even though he didn't live there. There was just something in the way he paid the pizza delivery guy, the way he touched his shoulder and talked to him, though I couldn't hear what he was saying. A gentle, self-effacing breeze wafted its way across the room to me. And the next thing the poor guy knew, he was walking me home to my apartment.

I guess it lasted about four months.

Until the day we found ourselves waiting in a long line at a movie theater. It was a movie you had to see in a theater, with lots of other live people. The year, I remember, was 1992, so, let's say it was *The Crying Game*. You had to see that one right away, before anyone told you that the pretty lady turns out to have a penis. Yes, it must have been *The Crying Game*, and it was downtown Manhattan; let's say the Angelika Film Center. It was a Friday so there was a sense of occasion and also the slight hint of hysteria you find in New Yorkers when they're packed in with a bunch of other New Yorkers.

We're close to the front of the herd but not so close we can see the rope being removed. But we feel the rope has been removed, because the mass surges slightly ahead. And then, we're off.

We walk quickly into the theater, and there are plenty of places to sit. This is our first time going to a movie, so I stand next to him in the aisle. I don't know whether he prefers the front, back, or middle. He stands, looking around while people rush in around us from all sides, taking seats. He seems oblivious to the time-sensitive nature of the moment. He seems to be . . . thinking.

Suddenly his laid-back quality, which had been so soothing, is life-threatening. Whole rows of good seats disappear in front of our eyes. Jesus, man, do something! I grab his hand and pull him to the last pair of decent seats in the theater.

This is not a man Darwin would want me to be with.

The relationship is dead in the water.

In the end, Transition Boy helped me through a hard time and gave me one more gift before parting—the certainty that I had done the right thing. I don't remember how I broke the news—but I used some time-honored version of "this isn't working out." To my surprise, he was surprised. He was quiet at first and then when he spoke his voice had a bass tone I hadn't heard from him before. He said, "You realize that now you have as much chance of getting married as you do of being the victim of a terrorist attack." I had not read Susan Faludi at that point—probably because she was still writing *Backlash*—and I thought it was a creative if uniquely bizarre bit of soothsaying. But of course it stayed with me for its meanness, as it was meant to.

And I was reminded of that old Chinese saying: Beware the gentle, self-effacing wind. It may turn out that the pretty lady has a penis.

Butterflies and Martinis

♥

Liz Dubelman

Ryan and I met at a bar over martinis. He moved in on our three-month anniversary and to commemorate the occasion he bought us this beautiful martini set. He was so sweet and thoughtful, but lately he'd been feeling so distant.

One day last week Ryan was out, which is my favorite time to clean. I like to put on his big Harvard sweatshirt, blast the Go-Go's, and when I'm all done I reward myself with a dirty vodka martini. I appreciate the irony.

That day, though, I couldn't find the sweatshirt. Or the Go-Go's. No matter, I pulled on a ratty old sweater, put on the Bangles, and set to work.

I started in the bathroom. I loved that Ryan used a brush and shaving soap. It was so retro. But where were they? His toothbrush was on the sink, but I couldn't find his shaving stuff. My stomach was suddenly infested with butterflies. A thought occurred to me: He's moving out. I sat down to make a list. If I found ten things missing, I would know the butterflies were right and that Ryan was slowly moving away.

An hour later I'd listed the sweatshirt, the Go-Go's, the brush, the soap, his Mets cap, his father's compass, his copy of *Atlas Shrugged*, his *Modern Romance* DVD, and his reading glasses.

Nine things, not ten, and that was even counting the brush and soap separately.

Relieved, I decided to celebrate with my martini. I opened the cabinet and saw something that made all the butterflies call their friends over: a single martini glass.

An Affair to Forget

♥

Maryedith Burrell

Unlike Edith Piaf, *je regret de tout.* Sure, when I lie on my deathbed dispensing wisdom to female relatives waiting to get their hands on my heirloom china and Fiorucci boots, I will probably chalk the incident up to temporary insanity brought on by severe testosterone poisoning. But, when the Life Lesson happened, I acted like a puma in heat and I'm not proud. (I have since learned that there are old episodes of *Designing Women* you can take for such things.)

Let's begin at the beginning. What are the two inviolable rules of dating in show business? (1) Never date a musician. (2) Never date a comic. Some people add, (3) Never date an agent to the list, but that really only applies to Fragile X blondes. Since I was a redhead with a college degree, I figured I was good to go. Josh McKenna* was both a musician and an aspiring comic—a double black-diamond dating run designed for experts only. I realize now that this was the attraction. The trophy appealed to my ego, so I trained hard and went for the gold.

Josh was a catch, a smart, funny heartbreaker who looked like he was separated at birth from Clive Owen. But, that's not all. The man

---

* "Josh McKenna" is a pseudonym. Any resemblance to an aging musician you might know who still thinks he's a player is totally intentional.

was a professional guitarist who could play like Segovia or Clapton depending on what was required. He was also mad for comedy. Josh's dream was to do stand-up like Robin Williams. He haunted comedy clubs and improv theaters. That's how we met. He approached me after a show one night and charmed the common sense out of me. The guy was A-list, toured with every rock star on the planet, called his mother on Sundays, loved his golden retriever and, more important, was willing to be worshiped by me.

I know a thing or two about worship. I was raised Catholic. To this day I'm weak for beeswax and Italian silk. Add bells, and I'll drop to my knees and recite the Agnus Dei anywhere. In my twenties, I spent a lot of time shaking off convent school and testing my ethics. It was that heady decade before AIDS when very little got in the way of a good time. Needing a man and wanting one were two different things. I was a sexual pioneer! But, when Josh McKenna came along, I thoroughly misjudged how powerful a combination of cocksman and catechism could be.

It took half a year for our affair to die. I spent most of the time house-sitting while he was on tour and ignoring tabloid photos of him with supermodels. I gave up my cat because he was allergic. I endured Sunday teas with his Junior League mother. I even passed on a job in New York to stay in L.A. and cook meatloaf for him while he was in the studio. The sex was so good I thought I was happy. I had bagged the bear. Josh McKenna was my boyfriend. I knew he wasn't faithful, but that didn't matter to a progressive female like me. I didn't need some medieval notion of fidelity to make me smile. I had a new meatloaf recipe!

My hairdresser, Kevin, came to the rescue. He threw a surprise birthday party for me at La Cage Aux Folles, a gay club in West Hollywood. The place was packed; all my friends gay and straight were there. The show was a witty lip-synch revue with a brilliant host who made clever jokes at everyone's expense. But, Josh couldn't take it. He couldn't keep up with the banter or laugh off the barbs. I was in a panic. My guy who loved comedy was acting like a sullen nine-year-old and the more I tried to make him feel better, the more he took it out on me: the drinks were watered-down, the sound system was bad, London had better drag queens. When the show was over and "the girls" called me on stage to sing "Happy Birthday," I looked back at our table and Josh was gone. Seeing that empty chair was like a shot of adrenaline after an overdose. My heart blew open, my brain kicked in, and I knew I was a fool.

Ever since that night I have employed what I call the "Table Test" for new boyfriends. One of our first five dates must include an encounter with a funny gay man. If my new guy can crack a joke with him and discuss the merits of Ultrasuede without squirming, we have a future. And, if I can make it to date five without abandoning a pet or pretending I care about the designated hitter rule in baseball, I will gladly cook meatloaf on date six.

I Could Have Just Dyed

♥

Kate Coe

B eing blessed with luxurious, thick, fast-growing hair—hair that
shines in the sunlight, hair that falls like an especially heavy cur-
tain of hand-woven silk, hair that entices random strangers to move
to stroke it—naturally, I've been cutting it, curling it, bending it,
crimping it, and coloring it since I was sixteen. My hair has been mis-
taken for that of Dorothy Hamill, Farrah Fawcett-Majors, Jennifer
Aniston, and k.d. lang. I've had hippie-chick hair to my waist (can't
eat soup, can play Lady Godiva), disco queen frizz (good in humid
jungles, bad on desert islands), proto-punk striped spikes (right for
smoky clubs, wrong for meeting potential in-laws), and an inch-long
buzz cut (yes, I'm radical, no, I'm not a patient).

Of course, I was blond as a child, but then, who wasn't? In my
early teens, I discovered henna, and spent a few years wandering
among the fields of auburn, russet, and Lucille Ball. Then, just like a
drunk who starts with Annie Green Springs and ends up with Ever-
clear, I shampooed in Nice'n Easy in Moon-Kissed Brown, Ginger
Rush, Copper Penny, Raven's Wing. I met my husband as Cocoa Bean
(dark chestnut brown), got married as Summer Berry (light reddish
brown) and added some streaks of Black Cherry just before going
into labor.

But once I found silver threads among the Sun-Mist Golden Brown
at my temples, I decided I needed professional help. "You get what

you pay for" has always been my motto, so I went to an expensive Beverly Hills salon, known for natural-looking blondes and lustrous brunettes. I met Matthew and settled into a long, happy ménage à trois of my head, his hands, and a secret formula of three shades of Miss Clairol. Every six weeks, I'd settle down to an hour or two of staring at *Town & Country,* movie stars, former first ladies, and richer-than-me west side mamas. I'd emerge, shiny, glazed, and consistently brunet.

All went beautifully until he told me he was moving to Florida. "It's not you, it's me," he said, proving that even gay men knew all the clichés of breaking up.

All for the best. I'd been stuck in a rut. My perfectly matched color was too matronly, too safe, too dull, I decided. I wanted to try something less predictable, less natural, more fun! And so, I solicited recommendations from colleagues, random acquaintances, and even, in a moment of desperation at the Beverly Center—total strangers.

On a tip from a strawberry-blond-with-low-lights writer, I met Cayleigh. A sweet girl with a semi-rocker boyfriend, rose petal tattoos, and a rent-a-chair at a salon on Melrose, Cayleigh said she understood my need to be kre8tive, expressive, and smokin' hot, because she was an artist, really, and sensitive to the needs of a fellow artist. She *got* me. So, she mixed up something smelly, slathered it on, rinsed it out, and sent me out into the world with purple hair.

At first, I thought it was maybe a bit much, but that it would tone down a little. My husband said my hair looked like the iridescence seen on corned beef. He's a chef, so the food metaphor came naturally. I tried to ignore him—he'd become accustomed to the old me. When I went back the second time, I suggested that perhaps, my new shade was a bit, uh, *vivid.* Cayleigh bit her lower lip and nodded, not meeting my eyes in the mirror. I felt terrible. An hour and a half later, I again went home with purple hair.

This went on for nearly four months until the day I met a friend of a friend for coffee. As I stood in the lobby of the Chateau Marmont, wondering which one he could be, I was hailed by a tall man with a suede cap and a British accent. Over cups and glasses, I asked him if I was easy to spot. "Oh, of course—your hair—it's really quite purple, isn't it?"

I realized that Cayleigh knew my hair was purple; she had planned for it to be purple; and that I would never be able to pretend I wanted purple. My hair might be rich dark plum today, but could become Edna Everage lavender tomorrow unless I broke it off. No need for explanations, no need for a scene—I just never went back.

Paul and I have been together since last Christmas, and things are going along very nicely. Once in a while, he alludes to the first time he saw me—"Aubergine, I'd have said"—and we both have a laugh, glancing at each other in the mirror.

Under Construction

♥

Debbie Cavanaugh

Together my husband and I decided to build a house and live in a small town with my three children. We worked hard on the house and then the work started slowing down, money grew scarce, but we were still living the life we envisioned.

As money grew tighter, I took a job while my husband decided to be the "stay-at-home man." The work slowed even more on the house. I didn't have bathroom walls or a floor or ceiling in my bedroom.

Then, one day, I asked for the ceiling to be put in my bedroom. I was tired of looking at the drooping insulation. So, my husband got to work on it a couple of weeks later. He put up half the ceiling. When he asked me if I liked it, I said, "Yes, it will look nice when it's done."

He got mad at me and said that I could at least say thank-you for what he'd done. It had taken him about two hours, and he had the children help him finish it. Something about the way he expected me to fawn over him for doing a bit of work after I had begged him for months to do it went through me like a hot knife. It sliced my heart in two.

Clarity blinked into me at that one second. I knew that I had made a terrible mistake with this man. I knew that, although it would be hard for both me and my children, I had to respect myself.

I started saving on that day to move out. Six months later, when I left, the ceiling still was not finished.

Smash Up

♥

Deborah Rachel Kagan

I'm in Brazil with my husband and it's fantastic. We're at the beginning of the trip and I'm treating myself to a massage. It's an amazing massage. Yes, the masseuse is a man. Yes, he's attractive. Yes, he knows what he's doing. His hands feel like a thousand petaled lotus flowers kissing every pore of my skin. Everything's great. I'm married to the same man for three years now. We never argue. We support each other's careers. We like each other's mothers. We like the same music. We pal around. It's great.

Toward the end of the massage, I'm on my back. And I realize for the first time in nearly three years, I'm welcoming a man's touch. My cells erupt in ecstasy all screaming, "*Thank you!* We thought you forgot about us." I didn't even know they were muzzled. What is this? A thin sheet covers my lower half. My breasts and torso are bare. I'm not embarrassed to be exposed on the table. I feel tribal. Primitive. Powerful. In this moment, I remember who I am—fiery, sensual, loving, nurturing, and sexual. The rhythmic Brazilian air chants songs softly in my ear. The masseuse uses the power of both forearms and hands to open the center of my chest—beating my heart into passion. Shocking my system into remembering. An ache, dusted and unfamiliar, jumps out of my core—I want to merge. I want to feel physically alive with another. I want to have sex for hours. What? Who is this? My eyes peel open, checking for shamans, witches, or someone else performing a spell. Only the banana trees and feral greens dance in the breeze. You don't want to have sex for hours when you're married. That's what I keep telling myself. Once you get married, you have good sex for a year. Maybe. And then, well, you're just married. You do it. But you're married. So all that passion and sass that you had, that you were—it just goes away. That's the way it is. Right?

Post-massage, I lay trancelike in the hammock on the porch of our Brazilian beach bungalow. I'm stunned. My skin is made of fireflies. I'm the full moon. I know a version of this me from my teenage years. Yet, this incarnation is different. Upgraded. More authentic. What am I supposed to do with it? Dread snakes around my ankles, creeping up my legs and making its way to encase me again. The fireflies burn brighter, engaging dread in a dare. Go ahead, try and stop me now, they flitter. It's then and there I know. I can't be married to my husband anymore.

We have three more weeks left on our Brazil trip. Beaches of Bahia, dancing in Salvador, romancing in Rio. I don't want my husband. Not as in, I don't want to *be* with him. We're amazing at being friends and advocates of each other. That's perfect. I don't want to have sex with him. I don't even want to kiss him. After four years together, I finally understand the missing piece. I don't have the hots for my husband. And I'm not sure I ever did.

What do I do with this? Can you scrap a marriage because you absolutely can't fathom or stomach the idea of having to perform any sort of sexual act with the man you're married to at the same time your whole being has decided to scream, "I'm awake!" Is this valid?

Struggling with this notion, I watch my husband in physical pain. He hurt his foot practicing capoeira (a Brazilian martial art) while I had my massage. A trip to the hospital confirms nothing is broken. His foot is badly bruised, causing terrible discomfort. Now lying in the hammock, it's clear to me. His foot took on the sting of my awakening. He's not broken, but our marriage is. There's no going back. As much as his body wants to slow us down, I can't stop. I have to move forward.

Handsome

♥

Bonnie Bruckheimer

I have had an obsession with handsome men for many, many years. I would let the looks of a man overpower any other qualities that he had if he was handsome. I was recently separated and on a plane coming back from Hawaii and this gorgeous guy sat down a few aisles away from me and somehow I managed to end up sitting next to him. And he was so handsome that I fell immediately in love—he didn't even have to speak. I ended up starting to go out with him and I knew something was a little off, but it didn't matter because he was so handsome.

I had a German shepherd who was having puppies and he told me that he worked for a vet and he was studying to be a vet and he knew everything about dogs, and as she started to have the puppies he was helping. And after six puppies he felt her and he said, "She's empty. That's it." She went on to have six more. So I should have known right then and there that the vet story was a little odd.

He told me he had been in the Navy and had just gotten out of the Navy and I never questioned any of it because I thought, Why would he lie to me?

He got a place in the Marina Peninsula and one day I went down there with my dog to spend the night and when I got up in the morning he was out walking the dog. I saw some papers and as I started to look through them there was something about a dishonorable discharge from the Navy. Then I started looking around the apartment. He had a couch that was catty-cornered and when I leaned over and looked in back of the couch I saw everything from my house. He had a whole cache from my house. I saw a guitar, a leather jacket that belonged to my last husband, a stereo—I saw lots and lots of stuff and realized, what was I thinking? I should have followed my instincts instead of looking at his arms, which were really incredible. He ended up stalking me for a long time. A long time.

Three Shoes

♥

Maira Kalman

I ONCE HAD A BOYFRIEND WHO DID NOT READ BOOKS.

I THOUGHT HE WAS SEXY AND PRIMITIVE

BUT HE WAS JUST AN IDIOT.

Tats

♡

Jan Worthington

Y ou'd think it would have been the cigar, the way he held it, caressed it, before beheading it with something that looked like a tiny, golden guillotine. That should have been a hint, but that was before two vodka martinis with three fat olives each.

A dusky, winter light fell through the windows of One Fifth Avenue and across the white linen tablecloth that separated us. He wore a camel hair cashmere coat that my mother would have lusted after, and wingtips that reminded me of an old boyfriend whose parents took us to Locke-Ober's every year after the Harvard-Yale game. We ended badly, but I loved his clothes, and often thought about them when I came across a man wearing wingtips or boat shoes.

I was eating one of those fat olives when he told me he had a tattoo. This was 1978 or so, before it was really cool to have a tattoo, before everyone had a tattoo. It was then still rather exotic to have one, so I was surprised.

"Where is it?"

"Oh, I don't think we know each other well enough yet for me to tell you that."

Uh-huh. A snake on his penis was all I could imagine.

I think it was a hotel room, but it may have been a friend's apartment that just looked like a hotel room. I remember only heavy damask curtains, plush sofas, and soft, pressed sheets. I had forgotten about the tattoo, at least temporarily, but as it happened he got out of bed to pee. When he walked to the bathroom, there it was. At first, I thought it was a big bruise of some kind that covered his buttocks. No, it was not a bruise, but all the characters of the *I ching* tattooed across his ass—all sixty-four of them.

"Your tattoo . . ."

"The *I ching.*"

"Yeah, that must have hurt."

"My ex-wife was a tattoo artist."

"Really."

"It was a wedding present."

"Really. Have you ever thought of getting it removed?"

"No. I like to remember the pain. And, it's a good conversation piece."

Uh-huh.

He fell asleep on his side. I studied the artwork for a few minutes and wondered briefly about his wife. Then I stepped over his Brooks Brothers shirt and his wingtips and left.

I didn't want to date a man who could only be happy by reminding himself of the pain he'd been in.

The Idealist

♥

Mary-Margaret Martinez

Picture it: It's the eighties. You're young and idealistic. And you're dating a porn star.

And even now, twenty years later, you're not going to tell anyone who he is, because they'll know him. Even if they don't know him, they'll Google him, or rent one of his movies, and then all they'll be thinking is, Oh, my God, I can't believe she slept with him. And you already do enough of that yourself.

So, you meet him at a party, and yes, you know he's a porn star. But remember, it's the eighties, and you're young and idealistic. You're all about how it shouldn't matter what a person does for a living, and that your job doesn't define who you are. (Which, now that you're older and wiser, you totally disagree with. Now you think that what you choose to do for a full third of your day-to-day existence does in fact have a lot to do with who you are. And if it doesn't, it should.)

So, you start dating him. It's kind of a strange experience, going out to dinner with a porn star. Because people recognize him. And then they try to pretend that they don't recognize him. Because they're embarrassed. Because he's a porn star. So there are lots of furtive glances and giggles until he eventually gets up from dinner and goes over to their table to greet his fans, and then it's just as annoying as dating any other star. You imagine.

Once, in a fit of madness, you take him to a family dinner at Aunt Dee-Dee and Uncle Dutch's house. You are mortified when you realize that they, too, recognize him. And they treat you like you're dating Tom Cruise. They take photos of the two of you together that they then develop and frame and hang on the living room wall.

And then, of course, there's the size thing. There is a reason he's a porn star. Your first impression is that it's about the size of a sixteen-ounce beer can. But you're wrong. In full bloom, it turns out to be more like the size of two sixteen-ounce beer cans stacked on top of each other.

And the sex? Truth? It's okay. Not amazing. Not that he isn't accomplished, because he is certainly accomplished. But you have to do a fair amount of deep breathing. On account of the beer cans. And overall, it just feels so . . . rehearsed. There's even dialogue.

"Do you like that, baby? Tell me you like that."

And you know you're supposed to say, "Oh, baby, you know I like that." So you do.

The whole thing lacks spontaneity. When you make love to someone, you want to feel like you're sharing an exceptional experience. Sex with him is more like being on an amusement park ride. Sure, it's fun. But you just fasten your seat belt and go along for the ride. And you're aware that pretty much every car is rocketing down that same track, if you know what I mean. Not that it's not exciting. It's just, when it's over, you find yourself thinking, I'm glad I'm not one of the people who waited forty-five minutes in line for this.

It's not like the two of you have a real relationship or anything. It's just dating. He travels a lot for his job, because apparently not all porn movies are shot in the San Fernando Valley. You take him to the airport, where you meet up with his colleagues: girls with names like Raven and Cherry and Destiny. Amazing, glossy creatures with fake hair and fake boobs and fake teeth and fake nails—they actually appear to be more Barbie Doll than human. And you're this Irish Catholic girl from Pittsburgh. If you had to describe yourself as a doll, you'd say you were kind of a Cabbage Patch type.

Sure, you feel inferior. And it's not like you're wondering, Did he sleep with her? Because you *know* he slept with her, and if you wanted to, you could stop by the video store, pick up a movie, and watch the whole thing frame by frame.

But you don't stop by the video store. You just go back home. Alone. You tell yourself he's just a guy who is away on a business trip. There are no late-night phone calls to tell you he misses you, no cards or notes or weekend visits. Which is okay with you, because it's not like you have a real relationship or anything. And then one day, while he's on location in San Francisco, you meet someone. The new guy is as far away from a porn star as he could possibly be. He's Mr. Clean Living—and you like him. You start seeing each other. And one Saturday night, he stays over at your apartment.

Sunday morning, while you're having coffee with Mr. Clean Living, you get a buzz from the call box at the front door of your building. It's the porn star, surprising you. He wants to come up to visit.

"Now isn't the best time," you say.

Being a man of some experience, he catches on fairly quickly. "Is someone there with you?"

"Actually, I do have a friend here right now," you say.

"Are you screwing him? I don't believe this! Are you sleeping with him?"

You try to get him to calm down, because he is, after all, screaming into the call box in front of your apartment building. But he doesn't calm down.

"Oh my God, you're fucking him? I can't believe you would do this to me. I really cared about you. But it's over! It is so over! Because I'm not fucking anyone but you! Outside of work, I mean."

The irony is not lost on you.

Eventually, he leaves your front door. You never see him again. Except on Aunt Dee-Dee's wall.

And then the reality of it sinks in. Your boyfriend the porn star broke up with you because you were too promiscuous.

Your mother would be so proud.

The Grill

♡

Jeanne Romano

I have always known I was never getting married. Everyone knew it, too, except apparently Nick, whom I met right after my fiftieth birthday. There was just something about him that made me not hate him and with that sterling endorsement, when he asked me to marry him I said, "Why the heck not?"

One Sunday we threw a barbecue party together. Nick insisted on making his famous ribs. All my best friends were there: Lisa and Dave, Melissa and Dave, Shane and Dave. I know, that's a lot of Daves. But it actually makes my life pretty simple. All my girlfriends have a Dave in their life, so much so, it's become synonymous for mate—as in "What's your Dave's name?" My Dave's name was Nick.

As usual, Lisa's Dave was holding court. Tonight's subject was the latest foreign film they had gotten from Netflix. We all listened as he told us about this award-winning documentary chronicling the lives of eight frozen embryos that had been stolen from the world-renowned Helsinki Clinic and eventually turned up in a Styrofoam cooler at a garage sale in Queens. His scene-by-scene re-creation of the defrosting offspring gave me a headache but it also reminded me I had frozen margarita mix melting in the fridge.

The tequila flowed as did the conversation. At one point Shane's Dave asked me if my mom had given me the honeymoon talk. To which

I said, "My mom? The woman who still refers to her gynecologist as the 'down there' doctor?" We all laughed, except Nick. Uh-oh, is this the man I want poking my ribs for the rest of my life?

Thinking he was feeling outside our little clique, I got him to tell everyone about my sister's interrogation. "Do you have any family members in institutions? Do you have anything that requires ointment?" Quite a buzz kill after you've shown everyone the ring. Then my sister hit him with her critical three P's. Personality? Paycheck? Penis? To which Nick answered, "I showed my personality, I showed my paycheck, but my Pablo only has eyes for my sweetie's Vava." I gulped down the last of my third margarita and thought, Vava? Eeew, he named my "down there." And, more important, why wasn't it my Va-va-va-voom!? As I watched Nick smother his masterpiece with KC Masterpiece, I had to wonder, Was my Dave going to smother me the way he smothered his ribs?

Just then the stinker of all questions slurred out of Melissa's mouth. "So, how many people have you both slept with?" I was hoping because of her bad grammar I could get away with zero, but we all knew what she meant.

Nick methodically ticked off his sexual conquests as he divided the ribs with a large sharp cleaver. One, two, three, four, five, six—slamming the cleaver blade right between the last three ribs—seven, eight, nine. Nine. Nick proudly announced he had slept with nine women. Nine? Nine women? To which I said, "Nick, I've slept with nine Mikes. And six Steves. And four Bills . . ."

Nick and his Pablo are now manning someone else's grill.

Norm Crosby Syndrome

♡

Lynn Snowden Picket

Sometimes you fall in love, and the object of your affection does something unexpected, and suddenly you feel all the love just drain out of you right onto the floor. Most people can understand this kind of instant change of heart if the loved one did something big and horrible, infidelity maybe, or certainly murder, but occasionally it's something quite small. Sometimes it's something so minor you can't even bring yourself to tell the person you fell out of love with exactly what it was that just ended any thoughts of a future together. Because if you did, you would sound, well, crazy.

I had a moment like this once. I had been dating a man I'll call John Travolta. Just to be clear, I'm not calling him John Travolta because he actually was John Travolta, I'm calling him that because he was, in many ways, very similar to the guy John Travolta played in *Saturday Night Fever*. My John Travolta also lived in Brooklyn with his parents, he was good-looking, it was the late 1970s, and his first name was John. The other stuff didn't match up so well, since he wasn't a good dancer, and his last name wasn't Travolta. Anyway, we'd been dating for a year, and he had actually proposed at one point, right in the middle of *Saturday Night Fever,* which is another reason it makes sense for me to call him John Travolta. He said, "If we're still like this," meaning happy, "in a year or two, you want to get married?" Flattered, I said yes, and we went back to our popcorn.

It's probably obvious at this point we were both still in college, the last time in a woman's life when it's still semiacceptable, if not technically desirable, to date a man still living with his parents. It's also the only time in a woman's life when a marriage proposal can be quickly classified as nothing more serious than a compliment. So John Travolta and I were sitting in a cozy little café one fine afternoon, and he said it might be nice if we ordered "a crèche" of wine. Fearing he would actually say this to the waiter, who might think he was stupid, or worse, that the waiter would think *I* was stupid, I said, "You mean carafe. A crèche is one of those little depictions of the birth of Christ that you see on people's lawns at Christmas." John Travolta gave me a stern look and said, "Lynn. I'm a writer. I play with words." That did it.

Years later, I told another woman this story, and she said she had a similar epiphany. Her boyfriend was telling her about something he read in a magazine, but said he didn't buy the magazine because he was "an invertebrate newsstand browser." Okay, invertebrate, inveterate, it's practically a typo. Except this woman could now only picture this man as a giant jellyfish, flopping around, getting the stacks of newspapers soggy. Another friend told me about running under an awning with a man she was dating to wait out a sudden thunderstorm. He made a remark about how much fun it was to look at everyone running through puddles while the two of them stood there, not with impunity, mind you, but with "alacrity." Her interest in him waned right along with the rain.

None of us told these men the relationship died from what should be called Norm Crosby Syndrome, named for the comedian whose entire act involved malapropisms, so there are probably hundreds of men out there who are confused about the details on why a girlfriend broke up with him. I'm wondering if one guy in particular is sitting at a bar right now telling his buddy that one minute he and his gal were having a conversation about how being divorced doesn't carry the same stigmata it used to, and the next she was packing her bags! Go figure.

In case you're wondering what happened to John Travolta after that day in the restaurant, I eventually found out he went on to become a copywriter in an ad agency. So the next time you see an ad that's kind of stupid and doesn't make any sense and you find yourself wondering, Jesus, who wrote this crap? it's probably written by the kind of guy who thinks a carafe can also be called a crèche. He's a writer. He plays with words.

Blind Date

ᦥ

Rachel Resnick

M y wrists still hurt from the cuffs," says Eddie Vaughan, rotating his wrists to revive circulation. This makes the tattooed yellow dragon covering his left arm jump through inky Japanese stormclouds. It also shows off his lean, vascular forearm muscles, which pop and bulge with the movement. Capable arms.

At this point, I don't think, Good veins. I don't imagine leather belts wrapped tourniquet-tight around his arms. Or needles plunging hungrily into that same skin I'm now admiring. . . .

I'm thirty-one. Eddie Vaughan and I barely know each other yet. We haven't wreaked mutual havoc for two screamingly long years we're together. We are on a blind date at the Café Tropical Cuban in Silver Lake when it still had waitresses with gold teeth and teased hair. Eddie has a fresh café con leche. He tears open a packet of sugar, dumps it in. Then a second packet. Third. Fourth. I'm mesmerized by the motion, the white grains, the excess.

"One sugar makes a Chevy. It takes five to make a Cadillac," he says, grinning.

When he does this, the white scar on the right side of his face seems to twitch. It looks like someone pressed two fingers across the cheekbone and seared the imprint.

"What'd Jamie tell you about me?"

"That you were an amazing painter." And a real man, with testosterone to spare. Don't get thrown by the distinctive scar on his pretty face, she'd said, or be fooled by the ambiguous glamrock look—he's a stud.

"She tell you I'm a convicted felon?"

"Must've slipped her mind. Are you kidding?" Too late, I remember this girl once set a friend up on a blind date—and neglected to tell her the man was a dwarf.

"I have two strikes. Worst one's for armed robbery."

"Banks?" I say this calmly, like I talk to ex-cons every day. Like it's the most natural thing. No way will I betray how much this unsettles . . . and excites.

"Mostly convenience stores, for smack money. We got caught robbing a porno theater when I first came to town from Texas. Out in Pasadena. Bad idea."

I pause, sip my own café con leche. With eyes lowered, I attempt to hide the surprise. I've never met an armed robber. Or someone with two strikes. Or an artist shortlisted for the Venice Biennale painting prize. For an hour, we've been talking about everyone from Lucian Freud to Tanizaki to V. S. Naipaul to Mishima to Kandinsky. I thought this man was a sensitive, passionate painter. Now I know he's an armed robber—and a former heroin addict.

"I love your tattoo."

"Covers up the track marks," he says wryly.

"Any kids?"

"I have a daughter, Devi. I named her after Rukmini Devi Arundale. Stunning dancer from India. Lotta soul. Revived *sadhir,* ancient temple dancing. She was also an early animal-rights activist. Loved collaborating with artists."

He guzzles the leche and wipes the coffee from his lips, which I notice are not only full, but somehow lasciviously so. The scar highlights his exotic cheekbones and the tilt of his slightly Asiatic-shaped black eyes. I remember Jamie had told me his parents were an odd match: His father was a compulsive gambler who sold textbooks, and his mother, a Japanese immigrant, was a housewife, a drunk, and a former bookie. "Now here's a story. Her mother, Kristin, looked exactly like Scarlett Johanssen when I met her. She was fourteen."

I blink. Eddie looks pleased. Utterly confident. He leans in closer. I notice beneath his polo shirt he has some kind of odd bumps on his slender chest, and I'm both fascinated and repulsed.

"She's the daughter of this former guru. An Indian visionary turned sacred chief. Her mother's a kind of casual mystic, too. Kristin had a bit part in this play I painted the backdrop for. . . ."

He pauses. I am hanging on the words. In the pause, I imagine the affair: the beautiful teenage girl walking across the stage, the man watching her, drinking her up like a leche. Her bathing in this gaze. Finding herself in his desire, and on that brightly lit stage.

"She got pregnant. No way I was going to jail for statutory rape or some shit. So I abducted her. Took her on a Greyhound bus to New York City. She had Devi when she was fifteen."

I raise my eyebrows.

"Fifteen?" I choke out, even though I just imagined the whole thing.

"Her parents approved," Eddie says airily. "They're more enlightened than these uptight Puritan Americans. Other countries, cultures, they're more accepting of children and their sexuality. A girl this age, in Cameroon? She's already an old maid." He grins.

I am surprised to find myself wondering whether Kristin is the youngest girl he's ever slept with, and whether maybe it *is* all right. Then I think about what would've happened if I'd met this man when I was a young teen; at that moment I imagine I can feel his body warmth radiating from across the table.

"Eddie, you're more well-read than anyone I know and you didn't even go to college." Books I know a bit; drugs, not at all.

"What are you, my parole officer?" Eddie smiles. His long lashes flutter against his cheeks. He's very chiseled-looking, smooth and yet male, with fine raven-black Byronic curls. He wears expensive rose-tinted glasses that sit low on his nose. When he speaks, he often peers over the frames, which gives him instant authority. So does his precise diction and his resonant voice. He intones, rather than speaks. There is something commanding about this man, even though at first sight I wasn't impressed. He didn't fit my predilection for either brash macho-man types or flawless pretty boys because of his facial scar and mysterious chest lumps. Not to mention that he's got twelve years on me. Now, after an hour, I can't take my eyes off him. Nor can I stop listening. His confidence, intelligence, and seductiveness are intoxicating.

I look down at my hands. My knuckles are torn up from boxing at the Y. I can handle this.

"Why were you arrested last month?" I'm thinking about his wrists bound by cuffs, imagining the metal cold and clamped around his skin.

"Some stupid clerical error, an old warrant from over a decade ago." I follow his cue, breathe a sigh of relief.

He tells me how he spent two nights in jail. On the bus over to county jail, he was cuffed to a Mexican teenager who'd stolen twenty thousand dollars.

"This kid couldn't think of anything better to do with all that money but bring two 'bitches' to the penthouse at Disneyland Hotel and get caught. 'How about travel next time,' I said. 'Out of the country.'"

I laugh, as if I understand what he's talking about. I can't stop glancing at his muscular left arm with its tattooed sleeve. He, in turn, sneaks glances at my chest. His desire is palpable, thrilling. I can feel him stripping me naked in his mind.

Even then, I felt Eddie was a true outlaw. I sensed he could offer entrée into a world of abandon unlike anything I'd known, a world of intrigue and darkness, of mystery, outside convention. He would be my guide, if I let him. And we would travel, be seekers. For what, I wasn't sure.

Looking back, I recognize beneath the romanticizing lurked an ancient pattern of responding to men with secrets. Men with parallel lives. Men who lied. I thought at the time, Here is a chance to enter that enigmatic world, maybe go where the men go when they leave. After all, hadn't my own father referred to himself as the main character in Thurber's "The Secret Life of Walter Mitty" when I was a wide-eyed kid and he was telling me about his affairs with other women? "You should know, I still live with my ex." Pause. "It's just for convenience. Don't get me wrong. Also, I'm moving to Thailand in a month." Eddie leans forward, looking at me over his glasses. "I didn't expect to meet anyone."

The intensity of his gaze, it grips. He's . . . unavailable. I am powerless to resist this man.

"Hey, I took the bus over here from West L.A. Maybe you could drop me back at the bus stop?"

A few weeks later, he will move out of his ex's house and basically live in his car. I will ferry him and his twelve-year-old daughter around town. Some months later, he will be back in L.A. from Thailand, making half a million dollars creating commissioned artwork for various celebrities and powerbrokers. These people thrill to the hyper-real paintings depicting experiences they wouldn't dare—years ago, Eddie made his name on a series tracing the graphic tale of his relationship with one of his hookers and her mother, then followed it up with a shocking suite of works inspired by his time as a teen male hustler.

Much of this new commission he will blow on hookers, exotic pets, costly watches, custom-made clothes, travel, gambling, and pharmaceutical-strength codeine. But I won't know that. Because while I'm attracted to the double life I sense he lives, Eddie will keep it separate . . . and secret, until the end of us.

That is, except for the time early on when he invites me to participate.

Ties

♥

Laura Cella

W hen I was an undergraduate I enrolled in an Introduction to Italian class. It met from 8:00 to 10:30 A.M. on Tuesdays and Thursdays. Since I could hardly be considered a morning person, my mother fairly shrieked with laughter at the thought of my actually arriving there any time before ten, but there were no openings in any other sections and I was feeling Continental. It had to be Italian, too—I mean, how could you not like a place that's shaped like a high-heeled boot?

The first day, I stumbled in, disheveled and grumpy, wondering just how badly I really wanted to do this, and saw that this whole becoming bilingual process was going to be better than I had imagined. A lot better.

The instructor was already in the front of the room, leaning on the table that functioned as a desk, arms and legs crossed casually, elegantly. He wore perfectly tailored khakis and an impeccable white linen button-down shirt. This alone made me stare. N.Y.U. in the early 1990s was full of black-jeans-and-leather-jacket-clad poseurs. Everyone looked like Lou Reed, including the girls.

Not this guy. He looked like Jean-Paul Belmondo—tall, slender, dark hair, dimple in the chin, strong forehead, lush lips, and one slightly raised eyebrow, giving him an insouciant, Gallic air. He smiled, exposing white teeth and a tiny dimple in his left cheek.

"Buon giorno. Il mio nome è Romano. Sono il vostro istrut-tore. Benvenuto al introduzione al italiano." I had no idea what he had said, but I was hooked. After that, I was never absent and smiled at him throughout the entire session. He must have thought I swallowed Chiclets whole.

Every day he looked more or less the same, sharply pressed khakis, crisp white linen or cotton shirt. Once a week or so, probably on department meeting days, he wore a silk tie. They were always of casually elegant design, a foulard or small paisley. I was dazzled. After that first day, I went to class completely groomed, too. I washed and blew-dry my hair every morning. I scoured places like Alice Underground for chic sixties styles. On a weekend visit home I even swiped my mother's last bottle of Narcisse Noir.

Eventually, my own sartorial efforts paid dividends. He smiled his crooked grin (I just knew a Gauloise should hang from the corner), and leaned over my shoulder smelling of something spicy whenever I asked for extra help. He was always very encouraging to me, marveling at both the construct and subjects of my sentences. (*"Gradirei il rivestimento di Armani nella finestra, prego. Formato sei!"*)

One day he asked me to join him for coffee after class. He had about an hour before he had to return to his office to grade papers. I swooned.

I had hoped to converse in chic foreign tongues but since I didn't actually speak anything but English, we talked like everybody else. It didn't matter. I was enchanted. We continued having coffee together nearly every day after class. Sometimes we chatted about our backgrounds. He was the only son of an Italian father and French mother and spoke three languages. I never really said much, just listened to the timbre of his sonorous voice and slid into gossamer daydreams about walks around the Tower of Pisa in the moonlight.

One day I got to class a little late. The lesson had already begun and since no seats remained up front, I chose one in the back row. He looked up and smiled at me. I smiled back. I could see that it was a tie day, but the tie wasn't one of his usual tasteful ones. It was one of those garish, technicolored Nicole Miller ties, the ones with fluorescent-colored designs on a black background. The design was pink and white. While I couldn't make it out, I could tell it was awful.

I had no idea what was the subject of that day's lesson. *Vorrei voglio* something or other, I think. I couldn't pull my eyes from the fabric strip hanging from his neck. It looked like . . . I squinted . . . Barbie? I stared and twisted my neck as discreetly as possible just to be sure. Barbie.

At the break midway through the class, I picked up my notebook *(il taccuino)* and tiptoed my way through the backpacks *(i zaini)* ostensibly to ask a question but really to get a closer look at that tie. Praying I was wrong, I approached. It was Barbie, all right. Her name was spelled out in big pink letters, randomly scattered with figures of the original ponytail Barbie, and blond bubble-haired Barbie, and shoes, those little open-toed mules that Barbie wore.

"Interesting tie." I gestured. "Gift?"

"No, I bought it. I wear it the first Thursday of every month."

"Why?"

"That's the day of our meeting."

"Meeting?"

"Yes. I am the president of the Long Island Chapter of the Barbie Club."

At the exact second that those words left his mouth, my infatuation ended with a sharp internal yowl, like a cat's tail caught in a door.

WHEN I GOT BACK, I WAS SO HAPPY TO SEE HIM... I WAS SO HAPPY TO BE WITH HIM AGAIN, TO GIVE HIM THE PiL T-SHIRT I BOUGHT FOR HIM IN LONDON
PiL
AND TALK WITH HIM, AND SLEEP WITH HIM, AND JUST BE A COUPLE WITH HIM AGAIN THAT I DIDN'T ADMIT THAT HE WAS ACTING WEIRD THE WHOLE NIGHT...
...QUIET AND I DON'T KNOW, JUST QUIET.
(AND LET ME TELL YOU, THAT GUY WAS RARELY QUIET.)
HE LEFT EARLY THE NEXT MORNING.
WHICH WAS ALSO WEIRD, BECAUSE IF HE WAS GOOD AT ANYTHING, IT WAS SLEEPING VERY, VERY LATE...
Where'd he go?
AND THEN I NEVER HEARD FROM HIM AGAIN.
I CALLED AND CALLED JAVIER'S MOTHER'S APARTMENT WHERE I THOUGHT HE WAS TEMPORARILY STAYING.
BUT HIS MOTHER (WHO SPOKE NO ENGLISH) COULD NOT TELL ME WHERE HE WAS.
AND EVERYONE ELSE, ALL OF OUR SO-CALLED "MUTUAL FRIENDS" STARTED TO ACT ALL WEIRD AND DODGY.

FINALLY JAVIER'S BEST FRIEND, TONY, SUGGESTED THAT WE HAVE LUNCH.

I found this place on Sawtelle that makes incredible burritos. Want to go?

IT WASN'T SO WEIRD FOR ME TO GO EAT WITH TONY. HE WAS PART OF OUR FILM SCHOOL CROWD.

AND AMONG OTHER THINGS, SUCH AS LOVE OF CINEMA, PUNK MUSIC AND ANYTHING THAT HINTED OF REBELLION, TONY AND I SHARED A DEEP, POSSIBLY OBSESSIVE, LOVE OF FOOD.

I'VE GOT TO TELL YOU THAT THOSE BURRITOS WERE REALLY IMPRESSIVE. HUGE! THEY FILLED THE PLATE FROM EDGE TO EDGE, SIDE TO SIDE AND THEY WERE SERVED "WET," MEANING COVERED WITH A THICK, ORANGE ENCHILADA SAUCE AND SOUR CREAM AND GUACAMOLE.

THEY LOOKED DELICIOUS AND TONY KNEW HIS FOOD. HE WOULDN'T HAVE TAKEN ME SOMEWHERE THAT WASN'T GOOD.

Wow! They look delicious.

BUT JUST AS I WAS GETTING READY TO DIG IN, TONY LOOKED AT ME AND SAID...

The Girl Who Cried Black Satin

♥

Hannah Rose Shaffer

There was no definitive breaking point because we both knew that we were doomed from the start. I knew, at least. If he didn't know, he wasn't thinking. And he probably wasn't thinking when he agreed to take me on in the first place, as his pet project, his charity case, his muse.

It was daring, to say the least, and the lure of something beyond my limited years of experience far exceeded a few good years of dogged common sense. Looking back, I can boldly claim ignorance. I can cry wolf from the mountaintops or cry bitter tears into a box of Kleenex beside my bed. I can lament the emotional growing pains of youthful naïveté.

Looking forward, I can boldly claim arrogance. "I know better now." I will replay this tired maxim like a broken record as another fouled relationship comes to an end. Looking back, I should have known better. I was too young and his hairline had begun to recede. I was too flighty and he was looking to settle down. I was nineteen . . . and he was old enough to be my father.

I'll never forget that first encounter. There I stood, at the center of Penn Station, nervously reapplying cherry ChapStick and scuffing my tattered Converse high-tops across the floor; an army-navy backpack slung over my shoulder and a head of wild, Shirley Temple curls. And then he appeared, swinging his patent-leather briefcase and click-clacking along in his Brooks Brothers shoes. The sleeves of his dress shirt had been rolled back to reveal too-tan forearms . . .

Had inevitable ageism not contributed to the demise of our short-lived romance, had we not been separated by twenty-one years of life experience, had circumstances been different, it never would have worked in a million years.

It wasn't the waiter who mistook him for a wealthy uncle or the woman at the beach who couldn't help but pry. It wasn't the disapproving glares that we received during our time together (even in Manhattan), but a basic conflict of interest that extinguished any potential "future" that we might have had.

It was a conflict of interest surrounding a black satin camisole. He liked it; I didn't. It was as simple as that. My fashionable sensibilities generally erred on the side of eccentric and thrifty. He, on the other hand, had developed an appreciation for the finer things in life: gourmet food, weekly facials, and women who could appreciate a man with deep pockets and an insatiable sexual appetite.

I imagine that the difference in years would have done us in eventually, but it was ultimately a simple black camisole that sealed the deal.

That evening, after turning away that posh little piece of fabric, I let him take me to bed for the last time. As I lay there, atop the designer pillows and Egyptian cotton sheets, I remember thinking at that moment that I was very much a little girl. In looking for a lover I had unintentionally stumbled upon a father: someone who would literally tuck me in at night and talk me to sleep. A man who wanted only the best for his little girl, even if she was nineteen years old.

The next morning, on a train bound for some place far less interesting and far more welcoming than Manhattan, I called the man who had forgotten, time and time again, to praise me in my youth. I thanked my father that day, although I wasn't sure what for or why. When I arrived back in sleepy, small-town Nowheresville, I threw my army-navy backpack in the trash. Every relationship, however brief, begins to play sneaky little tricks on the psyche. Now, I don't really know what it means to grow up, and I never realize that I've compromised my integrity until all is said and done, but if I know anything, I know that I'll never, ever be a black satin camisole kind of girl.

Swedish Meatball

♡

Monica Johnson

My advice is something every girl who has ever read *Cosmo* knows, but let me say it again. It's that important. Don't meet someone on the rebound. Especially not the big rebound. Rebounding from Death. I was a young widow. If you have to be a widow, young is better, but still not great.

I don't remember how many months had passed before I went on the first date. My friend was sick of consoling me and fixed me up with a guy from her yoga class. My first thought: gay. When he picked me up, he wasn't wearing perfume—that was good. And he was tall and cute. I wore my very uncomfortable contacts. I would spring the glasses on him later. He was soft-spoken. From Sweden. Linköping. He was learning the sitar and worked in a library during the day. In spite of all this, he wasn't gay. He bartended on the weekend when he wasn't too depressed.

I liked that he took charge and picked the restaurant, though theme restaurants were not really my thing. But if I was ever going to be open to new experiences, changes, then I should be open to Buffalo Bill's.

His heavy accent was intriguing, even though conversation was a little slow taking off. I didn't really relate to his experiences in Sweden. Or to anyone who skis. But having just come out of a sudden death, I thought of a subject we could both enjoy. Suicide. I remembered reading that suicide was the national sport in Sweden. I told him this and he laughed. I liked him for getting the joke.

I felt things were going well. He got quiet but even that was okay. He ordered buffalo wings and beer. Again silence. He looked like he could commit suicide right there at the table. I regretted bringing it up. And changed the subject to pets, dogs. It seemed safe but sadly it only made things worse. He looked so sad. I made a mental note to make sure there were no sharp objects.

"Are you okay?" I asked. He nodded. His dog committed suicide a month ago. "I'm so sorry," I said, "but how can a dog commit suicide? Are you sure?" He told me how the dog lost his best friend, a squirrel in the park, and for no reason ran into the street. I felt horrible. I tried to cheer him up by saying it was probably just an accident. He threw down his fork. "It was a suicide," he said, with such force that I shook my head and made up a story on the spot of a friend of mine whose cat had done just that.

"So let's go," he exclaimed. "I don't like it here anymore." I couldn't have agreed more. Nothing was worse than this restaurant, except the place it was located—Universal City Walk, Disneyland for thinner people.

It was full of people I hate. But again, I needed change. A new life that couldn't be compared to my old life. A life opposite to anything I ever liked. Good plan.

We walked around. I forced myself to fake happiness. I remember I read somewhere that fake happiness becomes real happiness, and sure enough, soon I was happy, just being out of the house. I don't think I'd been out of my house in seven months. The only person I allowed in my world was my doctor—Dr. Phil, every day at three.

Real air, real light, real people . . . all scary. But soon I was breathing it all in happily. It wasn't just my husband who died, I'd died, too. Now I was given a second chance to live, and live as someone new. Someone I wouldn't have liked as the old me. I never even liked blonds. Great! Right track!

I was starting to like my date. He was sort of funny, at least I think he was. I often confuse mental illness with other things, like genius, or a great sense of humor. I wasn't sure, but half the time I thought he was joking. Somehow we got around to the subject of cancer. Mine. He was overly interested, I thought. Wanted details. I told him I'd blocked a lot of the details because it was such a horrible situation. My ovaries were removed at age twenty-eight. Again, tears were forming in his eyes. He gave me a big Nordic hug.

"A cancer survivor! You are a cancer survivor." "Yes," I told him. "We are a special revered group. We get 10 percent off movie tickets. And various other benefits." He laughed such a good laugh, when he wasn't sad. He got excited and told me he wanted to get me a little something at one of the City Walk boutiques. He said, "Close your eyes," and he returned with a pack of facial blotters. Sure, they had a Victorian cover, but it was so bizarre I took it as him having a great and brave sense of humor. I laughed, but he didn't, he just took a sheet of the blotter paper and dabbed my dripping face. "I know about menopause," he said. "My mother has it." Okay, maybe this was an "I love you no matter how you look" kind of thing. I imagined Swedes would be that way. They had much bigger things to mull over. The things that made them suicidal. I gave him the benefit of the doubt and thanked him.

I was really falling for him when he turned out to have good pot. After a few joints driving around in his car, I saw how really beautiful he was. And he was sent to me to save me. He was so kind. I wanted to see him again. He kissed me when we got home, and held me for an exceptionally long time. He told me I reminded him of his mother and how much he missed her.

On the second date I was looser. I had crossed the widow line, and I wasn't so nervous, so desperate. I allowed myself to wear my glasses. He should know me. If he accepted my sweaty-faced menopause on the first date, I was sure glasses would be nothing. In fact he liked them, and I could see much more clearly without my eyes clouding up from contacts. But maybe it was a bad idea. The big new Cadillac I thought he was driving became a big old Mercury. The great tan was freckles. It was a Cinderella pumpkin moment. But he was still a prince.

The dates just kept coming. I was falling for him, even though he had a way of shaking a big mane of blond hair out of his eyes like seventies icon Farrah Fawcett. Every time he did it I thought of her and Ryan and their troubled kids. I couldn't help it. I tried to focus on how truly beautiful he was. Sometimes annoying, too, but then who isn't?

We had sex on the third date. Before he jumped on me, he literally beat his chest and raised his fist to the sky. I was worried what the fist was going to be used for, but he was completely normal sexually. Normal and wonderful. We found something we shared beyond sorrow, though he cried after he came. I was thrilled that it was a sign of how beautiful it was, and not a suicide moment. I was getting used to those moments. It was just part of being him. Plus constantly wiping his tears made me forget about my own, and that was great. He became a Viking fantasy. He had a beautiful sculpted body. I almost expected him to put on one of those hats with the horns that opera singers and Vikings wore. He was so passionate, and spoke to me in Swedish, it was nice but it made me think of smorgasbord, but only for a minute. Then he took over as a sexual god.

For weeks I was in the delusional bubble, seeing everything through pink soapsuds. The hair flip was flirtatious now. Sexy even. I didn't think of Farrah anymore, I thought of him and our first night at the Days End. I was in love. And it was a love my dead husband would approve of because I didn't love the new guy anywhere near as much as I loved the dead one. His accent made me tingle. I didn't want to fall for him but I did. So much so that I started to obsess that he would kill himself and I would miss him terribly.

Another of my men dead. I comforted myself with something I've learned from my own tragedies. Life is for the moment. I know people always say it, but to live it is hard. I forced it. I went with his mood swings and stopped questioning where it would lead.

In the face of his dark side this seemed part of the excitement. I no longer comforted him, I just cried with him. Other boyfriends might have run away. Others have. But he was a dark prince with blond hair.

His dark side and mine formed a bond. We saw sad movies together. But after a while, I felt my own sorrow was enabling him. I would do a complete turnaround and focus on comedy. Instead of renting *Ghost*, I rented *Airplane!* He'd never heard of *Airplane!* He thought it was an aviation tragedy. Of course he did. However, he was very receptive and we were laughing. Okay, sex, laughs . . . not bad.

It couldn't sustain us through the rainy season, though. The clouds, the rain, the gloom brought all the depression and sadness right back to us. Well, to him. I was getting to the point where I couldn't be sad 24/7. Maybe that was why he was sent to me. To teach that lesson. But while it was happening I wasn't thinking that, I was only thinking about how I would handle the paramedics if he overdosed on our newly discovered happiness. But even that couldn't mask the rain and gloom. I suggested we needed sunshine, heat, and fun. A drive to Las Vegas. Drive there and boy, did I have the tape for the drive.

Bob Evans's book had just come out, and the tape took us all the way to Vegas. I don't think my Swede understood any of it, but he was happy and I was laughing, so high on his great pot. I could barely drive. We checked into the hotel giggling all the way. Vegas, the city of love.

Our room was on floor thirty-four, high above the strip, and we were able to look down at the lights. Of course he mentioned it would be a wonderful place to jump from. I quickly turned on the TV and looked for sitcoms. Thank God for *Everybody Loves Raymond.*

He'd never made love with the TV on, and he really liked it. Another plus, because I never turned it off at home. The light, the drone of sound has gotten me through many times.

We had sex, ordered room service, watched TV, had more sex, ate more food, watched more TV. We didn't even go down to the casino.

He called his mother in Sweden, and they both cried because he was in love. He was in love with me. I wasn't sure what I felt but even if it wasn't love it was still better than anything I'd felt for seven months. I got on the phone with his mother. She didn't speak English but I could tell she was happy. She sniffled, he sniffled, and then he hung up.

"Do you know what I said to her in Swedish?" he asked.

"No," I said, "but was it sad?"

"Yes, it was sad because I'm leaving my young life behind [oh, no] and I want you to be part of the new me. I want to marry you." Marry him? I'd only known him for five months and one of those was great. So why not? Marriages have been built on lesser foundations than suicide and *Everybody Loves Raymond*. It seemed like a good idea.

We got the phone book. It was amazing how many places there were to get married, and how many Elvises to marry you. I thought Elvis was a little passé. He was looking for a Sylvia Plath chapel, I think. When I bought the dress in the hotel dress shop, I started to think about Bob. My husband, the one I buried not so long ago. I teared up in the shop and told the salesgirl I was getting married. Usually, she said, that happens at the divorce. She showed me black dresses.

There was the license to get. If ever you have doubts about someone you love, take them to a bureaucratic situation and see how they perform. He was helpless. He couldn't deal with anything like that, but I did. He loved it. He found someone to fight his battles. I found out he was weak. He wouldn't get us a good table. He wouldn't make sure we had the best room. I couldn't help it, these things mattered. It was mainly in my mind. It was so Bob. He was so sexy though. And really loved me. But . . .

We made love for the thirtieth time since we checked in and I looked in the book for the fastest chapel we could get to there. Why wait, he reasoned, we could be dead tomorrow.

Yes! That's the proposal I needed! Every girl wants that.

We picked up the phone book again. I found the perfect, fun wedding chapel. You didn't even need a new dress. It was a drive-through. We both laughed and even ordered the extra Elvis. The strip was very crowded and we crawled to the chapel. The whole way I was questioning my decision. I kept weighing it. Live for the moment, or run away quickly?

We finally made it to the chapel. We looked at each other, smiled and said we were ready. We could even see the Elvis standing at the drive-through window.

No. Yes. No. Yes.

But my answer came the moment his car stalled in the chapel driveway. He kept trying to start it, and the gears would just grind. It happened a few times when one of the Elvises ran over and said they had a chapel Cadillac we could use for the ceremony. I looked over at him struggling to start the car, and at the three-hundred-pound Hispanic Elvis, and that's when I knew the relationship was over. We both knew. A few tears and that was the end of it. I asked both Elvises to give us a jump-start or tow us to the gas station.

Several years later I read in the paper that scientists had declared January 24 as the most depressing day of the year. Of course it was. And it could have been my wedding anniversary. Instead I was at Tito's having a burrito and never happier.

Thud

♡

Lisa Napoli

I knew it was over with T. when I had my key in his front door at seven in the morning, and felt the full weight of his body against it as I turned. I had been calling him all night, frantically, suspicious. Unable to sleep, propelled by mania, I threw a sweater over my head, slipped on clogs, and ran the six blocks to his house in my pajamas. He hadn't answered at work. He hadn't answered at home. He hadn't responded to a countless barrage of beeps. These were the days before everyone carried a cell phone. T. was a lot of things, but he was not usually someone who was out of touch for very long.

My instinct told me something was terribly wrong. Not that he was dead, or even ill, not that kind of terribly wrong. The human barrier behind the door of his apartment in Dupont Circle confirmed my suspicion. And if that wasn't enough, the voice that bellowed from the second floor of the duplex was: "T., what's wrong? What's going on?"

The voice was female. I had been hearing for weeks about some ex-girlfriend. Let's call her Darla. Somehow, for some reason, she'd been calling T. again. Somehow, for some reason, the tone of voice T. used to describe Darla suggested she was not some distant memory, fond or otherwise. Somehow, the backstory on Darla that she was currently involved with some elected official didn't compensate for that tone of voice, or T.'s unsolicited proclamation that he had no interest in her.

Somehow, when I heard that query from up the stairs, I knew that it was Darla. I heard a growl from behind the door.

"Go away," T. said, attempting to sound menacing.

"No, I will not go away. Let me in," I said, attempting to sound shrill. After a few rounds of this back and forth, a neighbor opened his door and said, "Shut up, please." I gave up and pounded out of the building after hearing T. engage the industrial-strength latch he didn't ordinarily use. I went to the hotel next door and started calling and calling and calling T.'s from the lobby pay phone. He knew who it was; he didn't answer.

After a half hour, T. came walking out of the front of the building, hair wet, tie sort of slung on, suit a bit rumpled—that harried look about him in full tilt. My mother had met him once and proclaimed him an empty suit. He had never looked emptier.

Paparazzo-like, I appeared in T.'s path. I started screaming at him, terribly unimaginative blather. "You liar. You asshole. You fucking asshole. I hate you." T. quickened his pace, ignoring me. On the streets of New York City, maniacs can get away with just about anything; even a naked person can go virtually unnoticed. In Washington, D.C., that early spring morning as the light dappled the trees in the world's most self-important city, people noticed this woman in her pajamas, screaming at this man who was rushing along with his head down.

But they didn't do anything. Maybe they assumed he deserved it.

Writing this now, it seems hard to imagine that I bothered getting so upset over this man. He did me a favor. Actually, it was Darla who did. She called me a week later to apologize. Said T. had told her he didn't have a girlfriend.

I thanked her.

Pre-Med Fred

♥

Amy Friedman

Fred was pre-med, intense, ultrasophisticated, and I spent most of my waking hours in my dorm room—the first to go co-ed on Columbia's campus—either making love with him, daydreaming about it, or hanging out and watching him study. To counter the clouds of thick smoke he exhaled from his Gauloises and Gitanes, I took up smoking. And none of that wimpy stuff for me—not those mild Tareytons or those rich-taste/low-tar Vantage filters. I went straight for the hard stuff—Camels, unfiltered.

This was, after all, Manhattan, early seventies. It wasn't just Fred. For a long time I'd felt I had to shake the image I'd carried to college—the Midwestern athletic, wholesome look. Everyone in Manhattan was dark, skinny, and pale, deep blue bruised skin beneath the eyes. So I smoked and drank, and since Fred was romantic and a grind, we usually stayed up all night.

But two months into this romance I woke up one morning feeling lousy. The campus doctor diagnosed a combination of mono, strep throat, and hepatitis. My throat was so swollen and my ears so clogged, he said I couldn't risk a chance of flying home for Thanksgiving; I might even miss Christmas break, he warned. Then he confined me to my closet of a room.

There I lay, waiting for Fred.

My friends were troopers, visiting often, bringing Zabar's chicken soup, bodega fruit juice, and fat, fragrant bouquets. Some of the boys were sweet enough to flirt with me even though I looked like hell and sounded worse.

I didn't flirt back. My heart belonged to Fred, but he called to let me know he was cramming for finals and couldn't afford to risk catching anything. I understood. Besides, he explained, wasn't mono the kissing disease? And how could he resist kissing me?

Friends were skeptical, but I invented excuses for him—pre-med called for real work, not like my artsy writing major or silly political-science minor.

One bitter snowy night, two weeks into the illness, five of my friends stormed into my room with a surprise. Somehow they'd commandeered a wheelchair—surely illegally—because, they said, I needed a change of scenery. They bundled me up in layers of long underwear, pajamas, flannel robes, woolly mittens, and blankets, and they wheeled me outside.

The plan was to walk across campus to another building to hear a concert or a poetry reading, or maybe we were joining a party; I don't recall. And the reason I don't recall is that we were wheeling across the quad from Furnald toward Livingston, my wheels skidding on the slick brick walkway, when just near the snowy field in front of Butler library, I spotted Fred. He was bundled in his soft navy cashmere coat—he was never a casual dresser—arm in arm with a woman I recall as being fabulous; in my memory she has glowing skin and a long mane of honey-colored hair. They looked like an advertisement for chic, desirable love, arms entwined.

Fred didn't see me—I was just this bundled-up ball of illness in a wheelchair—and I knew he would phone in the morning to see how I was doing. I just wasn't sure I'd answer.

Signs of Doom

♡

MaryJane Morrison

H is name was Doom and he had the kind of self-confidence that, in hindsight, was totally uncalled for. He was only a little bit handsome: tall, soft brown hair, and the kind of large brown eyes that don't immediately make you think of a predator. In addition to his average looks, Doom seemed to have lots of ideas, and often talked about different "schools of thought." Also, he knew some words that I didn't. I thought he was probably a genius.

I met Doom at a Halloween party. I was scantily dressed as some sort of sexual stereotype. He did not appear to be in costume, but said he was dressed as a drug dealer, then offered me the most devastating pot I'd ever smoked. "How witty," I thought.

Drugs were his "thing," Doom said. And I think his frankness kind of put me off the scent. I mean, if he'd been hiding his stash, I likely would have zeroed in on the problem like an afterschool special. But when he just announced, matter-of-factly, that he really liked pot, and hash, and acid, and speed, and meth, and coke, well . . . it kind of seemed like, I don't know, everybody has a hobby. I shouldn't be so judgy.

Plus, we were having so much sex, it was hard to think.

I probably should have seen how hopeless things were with Doom the night he showed up at my college apartment with a sheepish grin on his face and a seventeen-year-old girl named Cinnamon unconscious in the hallway behind him.

He'd met her at a club and split some exotic drugs with her. Cinnamon passed out. Then threw up. (Sometimes the order of things is *so* key.)

To describe Doom as simply unrepentant that night would be to miss the strange optimism that carried him along in so many of his misadventures. For example, he encouraged me to see his behavior as chivalrous (he hadn't left her on the curb), and polite (he'd split the dope, instead of letting her overdose on the whole thing). For my part, I was mad about the puke (and irritated that Cinnamon was thinner than me). Doom seemed hopeful at the prospect of a three-way.

Weirdly, it wasn't any of that, that ended my affair with Doom. It was body piercing. He came home one night with a pierced nipple. Now, I'm not a prude about such things. My motto is: "Staple whatever you like." But when Doom opened his shirt to show me his new hardware, he suddenly seemed different. And if I had to say exactly what had changed, it would be this: He seemed shorter. Strangely, the piercing made him seem smaller. Diminished. As if the ring had pierced and deflated Doom himself. His swagger and confidence suddenly seemed silly and a little sad. And that was it. I knew we would never work. In the flash of a cubic zirconia nipple ring, I knew things were doomed with Doom.

The Forty-Year-Old Loser

♥

Amy Wruble

W hen I turned thirty-six, I decided to give up young men. I wanted to date a real grown-up: someone with a profession, someone who read the newspaper, someone who didn't have roommates and a three-foot glass bong. Sure, dating a guy in his forties might mean giving up six-pack abs and doing it three times a night, but it was time to grow up and settle down.

Steven seemed like the perfect entrée into the world of mature relationships. He ran his own business, had recently ended things with a live-in girlfriend of five years, wanted kids, and at forty was still boyishly handsome, with most of his original curly brown hair. On our first date, he impressed me with his knowledge of fine wines. On our third date, he cooked me dinner on the spectacular patio outside his beachfront home. It was such a romantic setting, with candles and flowers and white gauzy curtains billowing in the warm summer breeze. When we kissed on the balcony under the stars, I knew I was in love . . . with his house. I really felt like we had a future together: me, the house, and Steven.

And then a short week and two dates later, he told me he had to move out. Turns out the beachfront paradise had never belonged to Steven, he'd just been squatting there a few months since his breakup, and now his ex, back from Europe, was ready to reclaim it. A disappointing development to be sure, but what kind of girlfriend would I be if I let it show? Cheerfully, I asked, "Where will you be staying while you look for a new place? I'll come visit!" He paused before answering, then confessed, "I think I'm just going to sleep in my car." What? "Don't you have friends you can stay with?" I asked, incredulous. "Or maybe a hotel?" My fantasy about us frolicking around the Four Seasons was cut short when he said, "Nah, I want to sleep in my car. It will be like camping. It will be fun." I pictured six-foot-two Steven folded up in the back of his Toyota, peeing into an empty soda bottle, and shuddered. I insisted he spend the night indoors, with me, telling him I didn't think it was safe for him to camp in his car. I secretly hoped that being "there" for him when he was down might be a bonding experience that would bring us together. Rapid relationship-building for the girl with the ticking biological clock.

Besides, Steven still had plenty of potential. When I met him, he'd been running a small consulting firm from home. I was so impressed with his entrepreneurial spirit. Now, a few weeks after he'd had to move out, it occurred to me that he'd left behind all his computers and business supplies. Even his office stationery and business cards bore the address of his ex-girlfriend's beach house. Carefully erasing any traces of judgment or anxiety from my voice, I asked what Steven was going to do about running his company. Would he look for office space? "You know, I'd been thinking about shutting the business down anyway, and maybe now is the time." And just like that, my new boyfriend was homeless and unemployed.

I stuck it out. He was still the sweet guy I'd met five weeks ago who always called right after our dates to say how much fun he had. At least, he was that guy until I received the following text message, which he sent en masse to his entire address book: "I've run out of cell phone minutes until August 3. Don't call me unless it's an emergency." Did the guy I was dating really just inform everyone in his life that he couldn't afford to pay his cell phone bill? Or was he just really cheap? I flashed back to a time when he had taken me to dinner, back in the good old days when he had a job and a place to call his own. Or at least a place to pretend to call his own. At the end of the night, as he unfolded his wallet and scanned our dinner check, he pronounced, "A perfect century," pleased with what he thought was a subtle way to inform me that he had spent a whopping hundred dollars on dinner.

I sat there staring at my phone, rereading his text message: "I've run out of cell phone minutes until August 3. Don't call me unless it's an emergency." I wondered, does breaking up count as an emergency? It finally hit me that my supposedly grown-up forty-year-old boyfriend did not have his act together. He might as well have been twenty-five, except without the sexual stamina. But no, I thought, it's not an emergency. In the end, I decided to wait until after August 3.

We Got Married

❤

Penny Stallings

We got married in a fever. We had only known each other for a matter of days, but we knew. We didn't need a long drawn-out cycle of drink dates, dinner dates, and weekends in the Hamptons to confirm that we had found our soul mates. When you know, you know.

And then I met him. Really met him. At a succession of dinner parties given by my friends. It was there in an otherwise amiable atmosphere that I first became acquainted with his views on race, gender politics, and war; subjects I had never bothered to sound him out on—what with my "knowing" and all. The marriage only lasted through a half dozen such gatherings—although we managed to, as he put it, "run out the clock" on a full year. He was a sportswriter.

We had found each other at a Django Reinhardt tribute at Lincoln Center that featured Gypsy guitarists from the master's home region outside of Paris. I'd gone to the event alone as I often did—a talent for which I am held in awe and reverence by my women friends. But I say better alone than having to bring someone up to speed on the genius of Django and his short, tragic life. On this night it would just be me and my fellow Django-worshipers, not counting the usual contingent of oldsters with season passes who like to have someplace to wear their jewelry.

The first half of the concert was everything I had hoped with music that sounded like an old 78 rpm, and musicians so French you could practically smell them. I was so blessed that I didn't mind reading the program—all of it, even the donor list—during intermission. Intrepid lone adventurer that I am, I still don't know what to do with myself during a ten-minute break while everyone else rushes out to gulp down cheap Chablis in a plastic cup.

Then from out of nowhere came Jack—my soon-to-be ex-husband. Would I care to join him in the courtyard after the show, he asked, for some cheap Chablis in a plastic cup? I would—and I did—and I found out everything about him (I thought) I needed to know. For starters, he was a man not a boy, good-looking but not intimidatingly so, trim but not buff, and he didn't wear tennis shoes. All pluses in my book. Like I said before, he was a sportswriter—pretty well known if you read about sports—which a lot of people must do given his adorable little 1952 MG TD Roadster and breathtaking apartment in a prewar building on the Lower East Side. As for his past romantic history, always a touchy subject with men of a certain age, his only serious involvement had been with his college girlfriend with whom he had lived for many years. He didn't say why or how it ended, but I filled in the gaps with an updated *Love Story* scenario—killing her off with a fatal, though not disfiguring disease. In addition to Django, his favorite things on earth were animals and Italian food. Oh, and he also played the concertina in a band that specialized in Gypsy jazz.

Our conversation flowed into the next day, and the next, and culminated with city hall nuptials the following week. You'd be amazed how easy it is to get married—particularly if you're not interested in the whole dress-and-cake thing. Really, it's just a matter of filling out a few forms and recruiting a witness. A friend if possible, but anyone will do.

Friends. I had practically forgotten they existed.

You wouldn't have known it then, but my friends are very important to me. In fact, I take great pride in being a collector of people—all kinds of people who do all kinds of things and do them well. Accomplished people like my friends were always busy, but I managed to stay current with most of them by meeting with a different circle every few weeks for dinner parties. These were always profoundly cordial events where the wine flowed and the conversation sparkled.

It's not easy to break into a social circle of longtime friends. It's especially hard if you don't even try. And for the first few get-togethers, Jack didn't make much of an effort. In an attempt to engage him in some relevant sports-related talk, a children's book writer friend of mine who specializes in those activist kind of *Iris Has Three Mothers* books asked him what he thought about Title IX, which, I knew from NPR, mandates that high schools and state colleges must fund boys' and girls' athletic programs equally. It engaged him all right. Are you kidding me? he said, his voice rising. Title IX was killing school athletic programs, he continued on at an accelerated clip, leaving nary a second for response. Boys and girls are different, in case we hadn't noticed. The idea that a girl's volleyball squad should get the same funding as the football team was ludicrous. This whole political correctness thing was out of control. Government meddling was leading to the downfall of the country, mark his words. By this point, the children's book writer appeared to have turned to stone. The roomful of people had fallen silent. And I suddenly felt myself on the verge of one of my sick headaches.

Three months and four dinner parties later, Jack had told a rabbi that Israel was a fascist state, a shrink that psychiatry is a crock, a feminist that a woman couldn't and shouldn't be president, and a teacher that those who can do and those who can't teach. He was even intractable about Django. Gypsy jazz was the ultimate in musical achievement. No other music was worth a damn.

Except for Django, Jack's bizarre worldview came as a total shock to me. At ensuing dinner parties, I found myself saying along with my friends, You think *that* about Iraq? You think *that* about gays in the military? You think *that* about *that*?!? He was especially adamant about how schools and government agencies should be privatized and how taxes should be completely abolished. The more he talked, the more he sounded like one of those bunker nuts who stockpiles shotguns and cans of soup in case of an attack by the ATF. No, Jack assured me, he wasn't a nut. He was a Libertarian. I would have been happier if he were gay.

Still, I wasn't ready to—as Jack would say—throw in the towel. It was awkward, I told myself, but it didn't have to be a deal-breaker. We all knew women who had bad dog husbands—the kind you have to keep chained up in the garage when friends come over. These are the grumps who sound like you've interrupted them in the middle of a bowel movement when they answer (and they *always* answer) the phone. And then you had the contrarians, the bores, the lechers, and that special breed who belittle their wives in front of friends and family. We'd learned to live with them—or around them. My friends would learn to live with my bad dog. The problem was I couldn't. I could tolerate a man with raging Tourette's more easily than I could a man who thought the jury was still out on global warming and that Don Imus had gotten a bad deal.

You'd be amazed how easy it is to get a no-fault divorce. It's really just a matter of filling out the forms—and you can get those on the Internet. Snap. I was married. Snap. I wasn't. Miraculously my friends had hung in with me through this period of lunacy. They told me I shouldn't feel guilty or foolish about the whole affair. It could happen to anyone. Sure it could. Anyone whose only research on her future husband was limited to a few wine-soaked gatherings and a Google search.

In looking back, I realize that the only thing Jack and I really had in common was that we both adored the music of an ill-starred Gypsy with a gnarled hand who existed for a brief moment in time: a time when a whole new musical genre could be created from the idiosyncratic technique of a single man. In a perfect world, that would've been enough.

Subtitles

♥

Barbara Davilman

It was the end of the eighties, I was twenty-seven, and disco was dead. It was time for a new chapter in my life so I headed to Los Angeles. Before I got on the plane, my friend Claudia stuffed a piece of paper in my bag with the name and number of a guy she once dated who now lived in L.A. "Yale graduate, tall, handsome, funny . . ." "Wait a minute," I said, "if he's so great, why aren't you with him?" "I like his friend better," she explained. Knowing how fucked-up Claudia was when it came to men, I knew this must be a really great guy.

So, I settled into L.A., which meant I moved into a Motel 6–style apartment with cottage cheese ceilings and a pool in the middle of the courtyard. I met my first blonde with fake boobs who drove a Beemer and talked baby talk to everyone. I bought a car and found a job, which meant I was now ready to have a boyfriend. It was time to make the Call.

David was, in fact, tall, dark, and handsome. And yes, very smart and funny. We sat and talked for four hours. I came to understand that the adjective *dark* also described his outlook on life.

We walked to the parking lot. He drove an old beat-up gray Peugeot with a can of Spam on the dashboard and a New Hampshire license plate that read, "Live free or die." Somehow this excited me, the girl from Long Island, whose county's motto is "Shop till you drop."

I think I thought about David for a few days, wondering if he'd call, trying to figure out if I even wanted him to. My four-hour date with the Prince of Darkness had exhausted me.

One week went by, two . . . three . . . I had completely forgotten about him by the time he called. "Hi, it's David." "David who?" I asked with all sincerity. He was taken aback. I was taken aback that he was taken aback.

For our first official "date" we went to some French place that had sofas and coffee tables instead of regular tables and chairs. Today I'd think that pretentious. Back then I thought, How romantic! We drank and ate hors d'oeuvres for hours. Finally, we arrived back at my apartment. It was two in the morning. I was exhausted. I just wanted to go to sleep but I didn't know how to ask him to leave so I suggested we head for the bedroom. That's right, it was easier for me to have sex with someone rather than ask him to leave.

What should have been a one-night stand turned into a tortured three-and-a-half-year relationship. I became a person I didn't recognize. I accepted unacceptable behavior. David didn't have a phone so I could never call him, I always had to wait for him to call me. "What do you *mean* he doesn't have a phone?" friends would ask incredulously. And somehow, I could rationalize this:

"What does he really need a phone for? To check movie times? He gets the newspaper every day. To yak to friends? That's what bars are for." After three and a half years with this man, I learned how to rationalize *anything*.

So what was it that got me to see that this relationship was doomed? Was it my mother who upon meeting him said, "He doesn't love you"? Was it that he only wanted to see me on Wednesday and Saturday nights? Was it the dream I had that I was giving birth to our child and he stopped off at the local pub to have a drink, saying, "She can handle this without me"?

No. Sadly, none of those was my moment. But rather, it was a beautiful Thursday morning, we had spent a really lovely evening together the night before. He walked me to my car and as we were giving each other little kisses good-bye, we noticed another couple down the street. Their loud shouts of unidentifiable words along with random gesticulations intrigued us.

We began adding our own subtitles to the drama playing out before us.

Me: "She's tired of seeing him only twice a week. She wants to see him more often."

Him: "He's fed up with her nagging him all the time."

Me: "She's ready for the relationship to move forward."

Him: "He doesn't understand what's wrong with what they've got."

Me: "She thinks he's withholding."

Him: "He thinks she's too invasive."

Me: "She thinks he's being an asshole."

Him: "He can't believe she's ruining a perfectly good day."

David and I broke up two years later, and I learned that subtitles are for the movies, not relationships.

Products

♥

Geralyn Flood

Before we start, I have to say this: I love artists. Always have, always will. Tell me you are a musician, a painter, an actor, and your cuteness quotient goes up about 83 percent. So with that in mind, here's my story.

I left my actor husband for a myriad of reasons (but that's another story) and found myself working in an office situation alongside a reasonably cute, metrosexual guy. You know the type—closely shaved head, very hip black glasses, and the casual but stylish wardrobe that lets you know those clothes and this man haven't seen the inside of the Gap in years. He was kind and funny . . . well, he laughed at my jokes, so that made me think he was funny. We started to have lunch together and over a meal of bad Mexican food, he told me he's a screenwriter; he was bumped from reasonably cute to superhot in about three seconds. One thing led to another and we started dating. And by dating, I mean, having sex with each other. We'd have sex and then he'd leave or I'd leave because, remember, we still worked at the same place and didn't want to be the ones who wear the exact same clothes to work two days in a row.

We finally found a weekend night where we could stay together and we decided it would be at his place, since as he said, bringing my stuff to him would be easier. Easier for whom is the big question, but I was smitten and so I lugged my stuff to his house. I'm reasonably low-maintenance in the world of girls—no straight iron, no gallons of makeup—but I do need a few things to get ready for bed and get me out of the house in the morning. Now, up until this point I hadn't seen his apartment in the daylight. It was always late when we'd get to his place; I'd use the half bath and skulk out into the night, blinded by my crush coma and visions of us at the premiere of the film he was writing. That day, full of excitement, I walked into the master bath and nearly dropped my toiletry bag in shock. Virtually every inch of countertop was filled with some potion or elixir for the face, neck, and body. And where there was floor space, there were shelves with *more* bottles. I was flustered, I admit, but I put my bag down on what space I could make and was determined to make the best of our first official day of coupledom.

We got home that night after a day of movies, debates, sexual tension, and well, we had a nice ending to the day . . . until we started to get ready for bed. He told me I should use the bathroom first so I brushed my teeth, washed my face, threw on the perfect "first night we are spending the night together" nightie, and climbed into bed. He hopped up and went to work. And I do mean work. Forty-five minutes later he came out looking like the Bride of Frankenstein meets Dr. 90210. His face was shiny and tight from some "nighttime renewal cream" and his hands were white from fingertip to wrist with a paraffin wrap. Thankfully, or stupidly, there was still a bit of the crush coma left over from our earlier assignation and I was determined to make the best of it. I leaned in to kiss him good night and he yelled, as best he could through pursed lips, not to kiss him because it would smudge his collagen lip balm.

I broke up with him soon after and left the company where we both worked. I am now happily dating a musician who, when he stayed at *my* house the first night, came with a toothbrush, Old Spice deodorant, a razor, and flowers for me.

Valentine's Day at the Psych Hospital

♡

Mary Feuer

No one ever loved me like you did. No one before. And no one since.

There was that time, though, when you told me you were leaving, because you had never loved me, not really, and never would. We were at happy hour at the Goth club on a Thursday night when you said it; we were both drinking two-for-one well drinks, but you weren't drunk. I was. We had been fighting all night.

"Jesus. Look at yourself!" you yelled in my ear over the din of some pretentious band. Instead I looked at you: at your compact athletic body, your sharp Sephardic face. Your white leather motorcycle jacket with its A for anarchy made you stand out from the Goths, and your hair still had a reddish tint on the ends, left from that time you dyed it to match mine.

"But you said we're made for each other! We're soul mates, you said!" I hollered, and the song ended, leaving me screaming over nothing. You shook your head.

You left for home to pack your things and I staggered out the door, blind from tears, and smashed my skull against a wall of white concrete till I blacked out. Somebody found me, I guess.

The ER was weirdly deserted, empty. I sat in a chair that matched the fifty empty chairs. The only other person was a frail man who was wheezing. They let me go before him, because I was making a scene.

"I'm too fat," I slurred, "I'm not feminine enough," as the young doctor examined my concussed head, but he was not experienced in treating broken hearts. The groggy on-call shrink convinced me it would be nice to take a rest and talk to someone in the morning. An ambulance took me to the psych hospital.

At the locked ward they gave me a pleated thimble with some unknown blue pills, and a paper cup of metallic city tap water. They took my shoelaces away, but somehow missed the Elvis Presley pocketknife you'd given me for my birthday. I could have slit my wrists. But I only wanted you.

When I called you in the morning from the pay phone in the common room you were crying, hysterical, sorry. You'd been looking for me all night.

"I'm an idiot," you said. "You're my life." You asked me, you begged me, to marry you, and this time I said yes, because it seemed the only solution. You said you'd come for me.

A ruddy-faced nurse came around with her clipboard to ask me what I needed for the weekend. I told her I was going home. It was then she mentioned that I'd signed some paper and committed myself, so only the doctor from my HMO could discharge me; he wasn't coming until Monday. She put me down for toothpaste, a toothbrush, and deodorant.

Mumbling schizophrenics and depressives with bandaged wrists played Ping-Pong and checkers in the rec room. It was Valentine's Day, so I sat at the crafts table and decorated a white plastic box shaped like a heart. Inside it I put decals of a bird, a flower, a pair of lips. It was a beautiful box. I was writing your name in permanent marker on the lid when I heard you calling me.

I don't know how you got onto the locked ward. I don't know what you did. But there you were, an urgent whisper from a stairwell I didn't know was there, beckoning me to run, run toward you. An alarm was going off. You took my hand and pulled me, down flight after flight of stairs. I don't know why they didn't catch us, but you guided me down, out of the building to escape.

In the taxi on the way home you wrapped your arms around me so tightly I couldn't breathe. My head rested on your shoulder. I gave you the box I'd painted, though the ink of your name had smudged a bit.

"We'll put our wedding rings in it," you said, and looked down at my laceless shoes. You brushed a strand of hair away from my face, and when my eyes, a little dopey from the pills, met yours, I knew, in that moment, you would leave me.

We rode the taxi home.

If I could find that box I'd put it on a shelf of its own. The last time I saw it, just after our only wedding anniversary, it held loose change, guitar picks, and paper clips. The decals were peeling.

I hear you live in Arizona now. I ran into your mother at the movies. She said you're happy, and that your new wife is Native American. I imagine her thin; I imagine her ladylike. I imagine her standing in sunlight on a bluff.

Still, no one ever loved me like you did. Not before, and not since.

Raw Sewage

♥

Kara Post-Kennedy

On our very first date he wore a T-shirt that read, "You Could Do Worse." This turned out to be true, but barely. I would like to give him an amusing nickname, as so many of my girlfriends do with men who've broken their hearts . . . cute things, like "the black hole" or "fuck face." But it is not my nature, so instead I will refer to him here as Les, which I think is both suitably emasculating and an apt homophone. Les was quite a good athlete and dancer and cook . . . he came from an interesting background, half Egyptian, half German, and he loved to read. We exchanged books as gifts and he cooked me wonderful and exotic meals. So it was not *all* bad. Just . . . mostly.

Les did not own a car but rather drove a paint-splattered motorcycle, pretty much the hallmark of a "bad boy." This may sound fun and slightly dangerous, but it really boiled down to being lame and quite annoying. After one harrowing trip through the streets of Hollywood on the back of his bike, we retired that concept and I just drove. Everywhere. To pick him up, to drop him off. Sometimes we mixed it up a bit and he just took my car, leaving me stranded. But mostly I drove.

I had a retail position at the local mall that, while not exactly intellectually stimulating, did provide me with a nice employee discount. But I soon learned that "stability" and "responsibility" held no appeal for Les; he was a true Renaissance man. He did carpentry, a little cooking, some catering, even a bit of TV work! (More on that in a moment.) All of this earned him income on the side. I use the expression "on the side" because Les was collecting unemployment benefits the entire time I knew him. I was young enough to think this kind of cheating-the-government stuff was rebellious and a little groovy because I could never do it myself.

Needless to say, there was not a whole lot of money to go around, so we did a lot of free things, some of which were a lot of fun, but many that ended up like the party we attended the night we broke up for the first and really only official time. Ironically, I have no idea what we fought about, but it ended in tears for me and him slow dancing with a complete stranger to Eric Clapton's "Wonderful Tonight." What I do remember is that the decision to end our relationship was his.

Believe it or not, I had not yet come to the moment when I realized with earth-shattering clarity that this man was not for me. It was not this night, nor any of the later nights after he called me to say he had become seriously ill; no, on those nights I cooked his meals and carried him back and forth to the bathroom because he was too weak to walk. It was not even the day when a dear friend of mine called to say he'd seen Les on a televised dating show, a show clearly filmed during the time that he and I were a couple. (I bet he used my car to drive his video date around town.) No, my moment came more than a year later. . . .

Although we were no longer seeing each other, Les and I would occasionally have dinner to catch up and talk about his current girlfriend (the trust fund baby first; then later the adult alcoholic who lived at home with her parents). The obvious weaknesses of my competition always made me feel smug. Surely the woman who had cared for him in sickness—after he'd broken my heart, mind you—would bear out, in time, to be the superior choice. His roommate would say, "This girl can't hold a candle to you," or running into his dear old friend at the grocery store I was told, "You are the best thing that ever happened to him; I don't know what he is thinking!" All of this gave me hope. Hope for what, exactly, I cannot say, but I think after all is said and done it boils down to my vastly insecure need to be vindicated and validated at any cost. When Les would hint around the idea that I was the one for him ("I always imagined that you and I would end up together"), I did not engage in banter. I would settle for nothing less than a full declaration of his love and regrets.

Alas, this moment was not to be; instead of roses and violins, my epiphany involved raw sewage. Let me explain.

After Les had ended his troubled romance with the alcoholic, he asked me for (yet another) favor. He had to go out of town for the weekend and would I house-sit for him and watch his dog? I saw this gesture not as one of "taking advantage" but rather of intimacy. I would be alone in his house with his dog and his things for a whole weekend! Was this the request of a man with something to hide? My answer was an emphatic *no!* This was an olive branch extended, inviting me back into the intimate fold of his life! I happily rearranged my schedule to accommodate him.

I arrived at his place in the late afternoon and was eagerly greeted by his dog, a lovable Lab who had been chained in the yard all day. I let him into the house and he promptly peed on the rug so copiously that it was instantly clear he had held it and waited for this moment when he could create a virtual lake in the middle of the stained, industrial-gray carpet. While I mopped up the urine with towels I would now have to launder, a stoner with dreads wandered in off the street with a dirty bong, looking for Les. When I explained he was away for the weekend, the stoner parked it anyway and watched me clean the rug while making bizarre non-sequitous comments. He said to me, "You know what's really weird?" Thoughts flooded my brain about the bladder capacity of Labs, but he continued, "The Earth is like, sixty percent water. That is a lot of water, man. And you know what else is really weird?" This time I thought, The fact that I'm on my hands and knees scrubbing piss out of this filthy rug? He continued, "Cats don't really have nine lives. I saw one get hit by a car once. Totally dead."

This surreal atmosphere should have primed me for my grand realization. When the stoner finally accepted the fact that I had no drugs to share with him and moved on, I gathered up the soiled towels to put in the washing machine. Being the Girl Scout that I am, I went into the bathroom to see if there were any others I could add to the load; do a favor and save the environment. What awaited me in the otherwise neat bathroom was this . . . a floater. Actually, a couple of them. This was not the error of not double-checking after a flush to make sure the waste had gone down, but instead a toilet that had been left unequivocally unflushed.

In that moment I knew. If Les had any thought in his head of wooing me back, he certainly would have remembered to flush his fecal matter before going away for the weekend. As I held my nose and flushed the toilet, a bizarre string of scenarios flashed before my eyes, scenarios in which a man who truly cares would forget to dispose of his bowel movement before the woman of his dreams entered his bathroom. Not one of these theories held any water or, um, floated.

The Unibrow Breakup

♡

Judith Dewey

What it basically came down to, sadly enough, were a few hairs between his eyebrows. He had a unibrow. Certainly not as inspirational as the Frida Kahlo kind of unibrow—no, not the subject of any paintings, no monkey on his back—just a few, maybe a lot more than a few, dark hairs connecting two bushy brows. They completed his face. A face that was handsome, very handsome, in fact. But I never really focused on those hairs, never, until they were gone. I never petted them, cuddled nor combed them; never even kissed them. I just loved my man, my hairy, complete, manly man.

And then he did it. One afternoon, without consulting me—but then again, why would he consult me?

We were in college, and we were lovers. Paul was a political science major. I was a theater arts major, meaning I spent the day doing pliés in front of a mirror, sang show tunes in the afternoon, and performed Shakespeare at night. I lived in a fantasy world and danced with men in tights. Paul grounded me, made me feel smart as he smoked his Marlboros and drank hot black coffee. He looked seriously at the world through his deep-set eyes framed by that lovely wonderful, stupendous, magnificent unibrow. His brow would furrow as he lectured me in politics, philosophy, and religion. And just when he'd get too serious, too morose, or burdened, drank too much coffee, smoked too many cigarettes (I do believe he was rather depressed in retrospect), I would jump in on cue. I would say something cute and perky, hopefully funny, and he'd look up at me and laugh. So out of character, Paul laughing.

That was my role in this one act, to remind him of the lighter things in life. Paul's role was to carry around the weight of political duress, religious oppression; carry it around in his heavy furrowed brow, so heavy, so weighted that it stooped his shoulders. God, he was sexy.

The day was like every other winter day in Michigan. I think it was snowing (and if it wasn't, it should have been), the flakes dusting the flat, boring geography of the Midwest. It was cold. The windows in the student commons were frosted on the outside from the chill and steamed on the inside from the hot breath of coeds. I sat in a booth warming my hands with a cup of coffee (I would rather have had hot chocolate but I wanted desperately to be a grown-up, so coffee it was), memorizing lines from the latest play. I was Helena in Shakespeare's *A Midsummer Night's Dream*. I waited for the intellectual, hairy, handsome angst to come plopping down in the ripped vinyl booth across from me, waited for that smoke-laden kiss, waited to be pulled away from my fantasy world into his dark, dire reality.

The kiss eventually came, the smoky smell at the same time, maybe a beat before the kiss, and then he sat across from me. His face looked odd, disconnected, off-kilter. His eyes open and lost, floating around like in a Picasso painting, not grounded. Was he sick? Did he have a fever?

"Paul?" I asked. "What happened to your face? It looks . . . different?"

He smiled. "You like it?" He raised his *eyebrows*—the disturbing plurality of his brows—raised them up and down.

"What did you do?" My heart pounded from the caffeine. Why hadn't I ordered hot chocolate?

"I waxed them. Finger-width." He held his index finger up to his face, filling the void between the brows. Much better, I thought to myself. Keep the finger there—all is right with the world with his finger there. Maybe, just maybe he could live his life with me like that, with his finger between his brows, until it grew in. A little eye pencil perhaps.

Paul removed the finger.

My heart sank. "But . . . but why would you do that to us?"

Paul cocked his head. The inevitable loomed over our heads like a bowl of Cream of Wheat on a cold morning. (Am I showing my age or do we all remember those commercials?)

At that moment, a guy in a faded red hooded sweatshirt and saggy jeans walked by. I'd noticed him before. He was in my stagecraft lighting class, the class I was failing because I just wanted them to light *me*, and I really didn't care how they did it nor feel the need to know how they did it. All of a sudden stagecraft guy looked good to me, like I wanted to jump him from behind and smell some sweat, some manliness, run my hands through his curly, long, dirty hair. Yesterday he looked Neanderthal to me, today a god. He would never wax.

Paul took a sip of my coffee, lit a cigarette, and did the up and down thing again with the new twins. "Study at my place?" He was smiling . . . again. Why was he so happy? Where was my brooding, angry lover?

Not knowing what to say, I started reciting my lines from the script. "Love looks not with the eyes but with the mind." I slammed the script shut. Bullshit . . . Shakespeare.

In all fairness to Paul, actually in fairness to his brows, I knew this was coming. This "break up" thing, this "it's over" thing, this "it's better if we see other people" thing, this "parting is such sweet sorrow" thing. It was inevitable. I was moving on to graduate school in New York and we were in Michigan. We'd been dating for a couple years. It was serious, like unibrow seriousness. The next step would either be marriage, or a painful breakup. Neither of us knew how to painfully break up and we really didn't want to get married, never discussed it. I knew he would stay in Michigan, would thrive as a small-town guy;

a small-town guy who waxes. I had big plans, lofty ambitions, and needed to kick my legs in a New York chorus line, needed to play the role of the starving actress for a while. The waxing made it all crystal clear.

We did go back to his place to "study." I relented but kept my eyes closed. I was busy the next day, sick the day after, and probably rude the day after that. I am so sorry, Paul!

Eventually he stopped calling but apparently kept waxing, as I would see him on campus with his bi-brows from time to time. And he did look a little happier, lighter, stood a little straighter. And I was happy for him, really. Maybe the unibrow, those few little extra hairs he carried around, was heavier than I thought. Maybe my holding on to those hairs, my unconscious need for his unibrow, weighted him down. Regardless, Paul found his happiness in an index-finger-width of wax and, forgive the pun, gave me a smooth exit plan to New York and my future.

The Cheese Stands Alone

♡

Darby Clark

Fifty-two and never married wasn't obvious enough for me. Neither was the fact that the only relationship he considered "serious" was the one he'd just come out of with a girl twenty-five years younger than him. Maybe even twenty-six, but who was I to judge? I was nuts about him. In fact, I think I may have even been beyond nuts. My heart swelled, my mind danced, and my body tingled at the mere sight or sound of him. I'd be lying if I said I suspected anything. I thought it was me.

It all started one warm and humid summer night. The moon was full and low, glowing like an iridescent orb suspended along the bottom of the sky. Although we were only on our way to the beach for the weekend, I was in heaven. It took a special guy to get me to step out of my life and into his for any amount of time, let alone a whole weekend. I found most other men boring.

We talked and laughed for most of the drive there, not about anything much really, mostly work, Bush, and people we knew. With both of us running our own businesses, being politically in sync, and having a handful of friends in common, we were never short on small-talk topics to fill the time. But when his voice suddenly became infused with a parental tone as he prepared me for what to expect over the course of the weekend, I braced for bad news—like the house was under construction and that there were no bathrooms for us to use. Instead, he apparently felt the need to *establish* how he would be doing "his own thing" and that I shouldn't expect him to hang around and baby-sit me all day. Great! I thought. That meant no one clinging to me. No smothering, no stifling, no making demands. Could it be? Someone who was willing to give me space? To leave me alone? Freedom in a relationship with a guy? Was it possible? Heaven just got even sweeter.

It was late. We'd been driving for hours, and I was tired. I dropped my head back onto the headrest and closed my eyes. He turned the music up slightly and tapped out the notes of "Sweet Home Alabama" on the steering wheel as he half hummed and half sang along under his breath. I was having thoughts of him underneath my lids—fantasies, visions of what we'd do when we were out of his tiny little car and sprawled out on his bed.

I reached over the console to touch his leg, propelled by the desire to feel his skin with my hand. But my palm had barely grazed the hairs on his thigh when he jerked it away from me, acting as if we were in grammar school and I was about to wipe boogers on him. (Here we have Red Flag Number One.) For a nanosecond I wondered why, but then told myself that maybe he just didn't like to be touched while he drove. From there I convinced myself that it didn't even have that much meaning and instead that I'd imagined it. With no time to waste, I erased all traces of question or concern from my short-term memory. Plus, right afterward, he lovingly patted my knee and gently squeezed it. "You awake, baby?" he asked. I took his hand and said yes. Surely there were no issues with my touching his leg if he had no problem touching mine. So it *was* me after all. It had to be. Whew . . . what a relief. Thank God. Everything was okay.

As we turned into the driveway, my heart began to palpitate. I could not wait to get inside and finish what I'd started in my head with him. He smiled at me and turned the key to get it out of the ignition. "Ready?" he said cheerily. I wasn't, because I had to gather my things, so he headed into the house first. When I walked through the door he was standing, holding our bags and waiting for me to catch up, seemingly postured to give me the tour. "Ready?" he asked again. I walked toward him, leading with my lips. I had one target, and it was to land them on his. The bags dropped to the floor. "Hellloooo there," he cooed. Within seconds, our clothes were flying, dropping to the floor, leaving a trail to the bedroom like Hansel and Gretel's breadcrumbs. What a night. I didn't know if it was me or him or us, but something about this relationship was different. I fell asleep looking forward to the morning, when I'd get to open my eyes and see him again.

Day broke to the sound of waves gently brushing the shore, birds singing, and the sun coming through the skylight like a dagger. We both stirred. He leaned over, eyes squinty and lips tightly puckered as if to indicate that I should do the same to receive my good-morning kiss. He pecked me on my reciprocating mouth and rolled out of bed into the bathroom . . . and then out the door. I could tell that this was where the limited-access program began. I didn't care. I went for a walk on the beach while he went to the gym and then kept myself busy pruning flowers and reading for the rest of the afternoon while he biked, swam, surfed, played basketball, and then jogged home.

From the living room, I heard the front door slam. He was winded when he came in and plopped down next to me on the couch. I thought about how much he'd love a massage after spending the whole day in his self-imposed athletic marathon. I looked at him and smiled. He laid back and let out a heavy sigh. "Boy, I'm beat," he said. I climbed on top of him and kissed his neck, ready to propose one of my famous rubdowns. He leaned over and leafed through the newspaper, fingering the top few pages and glancing at the headings.

I breathed in to start to say that I had his favorite massage oil in my bag but stopped because he looked confused. His body tensed up and he pulled back before I could say anything. Was it my breath? If it was, that's not what he said. He said, "I can't read the paper with you on top of me," and nudged me off. (This was Red Flag Number Two.)

Apparently, there was a schedule during which he would make himself available to make love to me, and for some reason it seemed to only be on the itinerary after dinner and before we slept. Any attempt to deviate landed me in the penalty box. A little quirky, but okay, I didn't mind. It was fine. Actually, I liked it sometimes because things could get really interesting when he let me out. Eventually though, I caught on that there was more to that routine than I'd realized. Unfortunately, I only figured it out once it was too late.

It was a few weeks before I saw him again because we were both traveling. Meanwhile, no matter how busy I was, thoughts of seeing him again were always on my mind. But by the time our next dinner/sex/sleepover rolled around, there was trouble in paradise, and I was taken totally by surprise. It happened when we kissed. Something changed. His lips lacked their former pliability. They were rigid and unwilling. It was as if I were kissing someone else—a complete stranger. He was controlled, not passionate. (Red Flag Number Three.) Oh, no, this can't be good, I thought. Was he about to kibosh the best part?

Shoot! Not another guy who is hiding another guy underneath. Not this time. Not *this* guy. I remained buried in the icy coldness of his touch, trying to figure out what to do next. The natural choice was to make love to him anyway, hoping that the walnut pit sitting at the base of my sternum would fade away as we heated up. But afterward, the pit was still there, and I wanted to cry. Although the actual sex was off the charts as usual, I could feel the wall that he'd inserted between us. So I took a deep breath, tried to hold my quivering chin still, and said, "Richard?"

"Yeessss?" he responded as he stroked my hair and kissed my forehead.

"I think we have a problem."

"Why? What's the matter?"

"I think my body and heart can't be separated when it comes to you."

"What do you mean?"

"I mean—I can't do this robotically. I really like you."

He froze.

"You mean you have feelings?"

"Yes."

Another lecture ensued. (Pulling up to Red Flag Number Four, and still not sensing a pattern.) Did he want me to say no? That didn't make any sense. Now, I didn't know him well enough to love him, so we weren't having *that* conversation. Nonetheless, he upbraided me.

"Don't go there, Darby," he warned. "I told you I am not going there with you." (Well, actually, he hadn't.) I knew he liked me. It was *so* obvious. So what was the problem? Where was "there" anyway? We'd been dating for months. Why was he with me if he didn't want me to like him? The next thing I knew, I was getting chided some more. "I told you, I am *not* open to this."

"Well, you are to some extent because you're here. Why don't we just talk about it?"

"I'll talk to you about anything you want, but not my feelings."

"Why not?"

"Because I won't be vulnerable with you."

"With me? Are you serious? Don't you mean with *anyone?*" He was too old and too single to get away with that. For God's sake, I thought. Not another one. What was *up* with all these unfledged guys? They were everywhere, appearing in pandemic proportions.

"Look," he continued, "I do not want the obligation of having to take you out to dinner every Saturday night or drag you to the beach with me every weekend."

Huh? *Drag?* First of all, what did our social calendars have to do with being vulnerable? And who said anything about going anywhere? Had it not occurred to him that maybe I didn't want to go to the beach every weekend? Heck, half the time I wasn't even hungry either, whether it was Saturday night or not. What I liked was *him*. I didn't care where we were or what we did. I would have been happy sitting beside him on a sidewalk on a Tuesday morning breathing in bus fumes. What was going on? I was baffled until I realized that he must have experienced a spell of momentary dementia and confused me with someone else. In retrospect, I'd say it was the twenty-five-year-old and all those like her who came before. He was stuck. We fell asleep enveloped in a light veil of awkward silence. In the morning, before we got out of bed, and even before my scrunched-up, squinting, puckered kiss, the first words he uttered were, "Ah, ouch, ohhhh. Your bed is killing my back." He was actually squirming. (That was it. The Fifth and Final Red Flag.) In that moment he turned into a hunk of feta cheese and I had trouble reconciling how something could smell so bad and still taste so good. Even so, I wanted to keep eating despite the fact that I knew deep down he was warming up to run away. I suppose I could have tried blaming it on his aging body. But I knew it wasn't rickety bones any more than it was my mattress. No. It was *fear*. Come to think of it, maybe that's what smelled so bad.

In the end he just drifted away, which was fine because I realized that this man would always live his life in fear, trying to control the uncontrollable, mainly love. It was then that I finally understood the line, "And the cheese stands alone."

Oh, How We Love Bad Boys

♥

Cindy Chupack

A good man is not so hard to find. I've dated a bunch of them. They call when they say they're going to call, they take you out on actual dates, they tell their friends and even their parents about you, they *like* their parents, they play their phone messages in front of you, they have just one glass of wine with dinner because they're driving, they have jobs, they have female friends they haven't slept with . . . yeah, yeah, whatever. The point is they're not hard to find. *Bad boys* are hard to find, because they're never where they're supposed to be. In fact, they're not supposed to be anywhere. They do as they please. They go where the wind takes them. If you're lucky, you might get a cell phone number, so you never know exactly what (or who) a bad boy is doing. It's infuriating and insensitive and intriguing and insane and oh, how we love bad boys.

You know you're dating a bad boy when you're not sure you're actually dating. Bad boys are usually one of two things: unavailable or undressed. This leaves you unable to think of anything but where the hell is he and when will he do that to me again? Bad boys are rule-breakers and heartbreakers and bed-shakers and oh, how we love bad boys.

A bad boy will call you "baby," probably because he forgot your name, but still, there's nothing sexier than a bad boy who's dying to see you, baby. It doesn't matter if anything he says is true. It sounds good, and it feels good, because baby, bad boys have thrown down. Bad boys are not tentative about kissing. They are not tentative about anything. They know what they want and they go for it, which is thrilling when it's you, and not so thrilling when it's suddenly the model (not) eating at the table next to yours. Of course, that rarely happens, because bad boys rarely take you out. They don't have to. The bar is low for bad boys. They don't have to surprise you with flowers, it's a surprise they show up at all. In fact, a bad boy is happy to let a good guy take you to dinner, ask you about you, kiss you good night at the door . . . a bad boy knows he can call at midnight and still get invited over for dessert.

Bad boys *are* dessert. They're like hot fudge sundaes. You know they're not good for you. You know that as a woman, at a certain age, you're not supposed to indulge anymore, but that doesn't mean you won't fantasize about it while you're eating your mixed berries. The other fantasy, of course, is that you will somehow reform a bad boy. That you will meet with a motorcycle and tattoos and a love of bars, and he'll tell you he's trouble, but clearly that's all a front. In truth, he's just wounded, as we all are, and eventually he'll fall madly in love with you because you are what's missing in his life. Okay, I admit it. I recently married a bad boy. The thing is, bad boys are so elusive, so aware of their options (her, her, and her), so impossible to pin down, that when a bad boy gives you a ring, it means something. That you should hire a very old nanny. Oh, oh, oh, how we love bad boys.

Bah Humbug

❦

Katherine Tomlinson

We had been dating three months when my birthday came around in September. I mentioned it casually once (well, maybe twice), thinking it would be nice to mark the occasion with dinner somewhere nice. But my birthday came and went unacknowledged.

For Halloween, I sent him a silly card that had a county fair theme. We'd just been to the county fair and enjoyed ourselves. He thanked me for the card.

He went up north to celebrate Thanksgiving with his older sister and her family and we exchanged some seventy e-mail messages that day.

Christmas approached. We had not yet been intimate, but it seemed like a good time to get closer. He had a cabin in the mountains and had been talking about us going up there almost from the first time we went out. It was beautiful there in the winter, he said, and I would love it. He would make pancakes for our breakfast.

One bright December day before Christmas, we went out to eat and I handed him a gift bag. In it I'd put all the ingredients for a breakfast feast: pancake mix, maple syrup, gourmet bacon. I'd added a packet of condoms and in the card I included, I made mention of breakfast in bed.

He said he was charmed by the gift, although he did not open it in my presence.

He never mentioned the condoms.

He went up north for Christmas, the unattached uncle, the extra at the table.

We once again exchanged a flurry of e-mails. I got a Christmas card from my insurance agent. I got one from each of my major clients. I got one from my dentist. I even got one from my veterinarian, although it was addressed to my cat. But there was no Christmas card from him.

New Year's Eve arrived. We didn't go out. He'd told me he didn't like to be on the road on the holiday. There was no invitation for me to come over to his place to usher in the new year with a bottle of wine and a stack of DVDs. (I would have made those little puff pastry things I do with goat cheese and herbs.) Sure, I could have invited him to my place, but I have a housemate and it would have been awkward.

I went to bed early, feeling out of sorts.

Which is nothing compared to the way I felt the next day when he mentioned that he'd gone out after all, in response to an appeal from a woman friend he talked about a lot. A whole lot.

He couldn't believe I was annoyed with him, and pointed out that she was alone and needed him. *She was alone and needed him.* Not like me.

Then came Valentine's Day.

"Happy Valentine's Day," chirped a little girl going down in the elevator with me. She was wearing a pink sweater with white hearts on it. She was ready for the holiday. Her mother, also dressed in pink, smiled fondly at the child. So did I.

"Happy Valentine's Day," said the courier delivering a package from a client. My friend Sam sent me Valentine's greetings. So did a friend in Chicago. A box boy in Vons offered a shy "Happy Valentine's Day" in Spanish.

But not a word from the man I'd been dating nearly a year.

Not a card.

Not an e-mail.

Not a phone call.

And definitely not a heart-shaped box of candy or a single red rose.

I'd ignored the noncelebration of my birthday and Christmas. Some people just don't do the birthday thing. And some of my best friends hate Christmas. My brother, for example, is a lovely guy who happens to be a Scrooge. We haven't exchanged Christmas presents since high school. But he knows I love the holiday and even he always manages to send a card.

I had convinced myself that my sweetie and I were just holiday-incompatible and that this incompatibility was, in the scheme of things, no big deal.

And then came Valentine's Day. I wasn't expecting an arrangement of orchids. I wasn't expecting a gold box of Godiva or a magnum of champagne. But I was expecting something more than nothing.

"It's not like he's a stupid guy," my housemate said, which was not exactly helpful. "He's got to know how important Valentine's Day is to women."

And that's when I saw the future with the clarity of Sylvia Browne.

Technically, I could marry this man. He was ready, and he was *interested*.

But every year, I'd have to buy my own birthday present. At Christmas I would get gift cards because it would be easier for him than thinking about what I really wanted. And on Valentine's Day I would have to avoid going into stores with displays of sweets and flowers and (God help us) teddy bears. Valentine's Day is not a holiday that's kind to single women; but for married women who feel unloved, it's even worse.

Our relationship struggled along for another four months. The day before his birthday in June, I sent him an e-mail with a silly message about not being able to give him the world but offering to buy him his very own domain name on the Web. He sent back a fairly curt response saying, basically, don't bother. I sent back an e-mail that said, "Well, I tried." He understood the message.

We have not spoken since.

I miss him sometimes. And then I think about Valentine's Day.

Gaydar

♡

Zoe Braverman

He is my best friend" always began my defense when friends of both genders pried and prodded suspiciously at my friendship with Brian. Girls would coo, "He is actually really cute," and guys would roll their eyes with an unconvinced, "Yeah, right," when I assured them we were nothing more than friends. If attraction was an electric current, the air between us was stagnant. If attraction was a heartbeat, we had a flatline.

I wasn't surprised that from an external perspective, we appeared to be an item. Sure, we talked on the phone for three hours nearly every night, but we weren't professing our love to each other: we were discussing career plans. Sure, I was the subject of many of his photo shoots, but he was an aspiring fashion photographer testing out a new lens. Sure, we would giggle in unison in class, but it was the result of a mind game we were playing on our teacher, not a cutesy inside joke.

When he was out sick one day, I volunteered us as Romeo and Juliet in our class play, and was thrilled to inform him of this through my hysterical laughter on the phone that night. I even convinced our eleventh grade Spanish teacher that we did have a turbulent love affair and that he cruelly toyed with my emotions, resulting in porous or late homework assignments. She gazed at my watery eyes, half sympathetic, half uncomfortable. Brian was across the room, doodling on his sneakers, oblivious.

Despite my best efforts in articulating why we didn't like each other in "that way," I was often informed that Brian and I would eventually get married. This was news to me, especially because his girlish tendencies and passion for fashion had tripped off my gaydar. But friends and family have that sly way of infecting your psyche. Maybe I was a cynic, I considered. Perhaps I was blind to the mysterious workings of love. Maybe when I was hanging up on Brian's 1:00 A.M. pleas for help on a two-week-late essay, I was hanging up on my soul mate. Though I shuddered at the cliché of falling in love with my best friend, and was queasy at the thought of marrying my high school sweetheart, I vowed to stay open-minded and alert for any signals that there was, in fact, something there.

An hour and a half into one of our nightly phone calls, after we had compared daunting to-do lists, analyzed the latest adolescent crisis among our friends, and shared bizarre anecdotes about various teachers; we had fallen into idle chatter. Suddenly Brian exclaimed, "Oh! My! God!" I readied myself. "Oh, my God, I love you"? "Oh, my God, what am I doing, why aren't you my girlfriend"? "Oh, my God, I am such a fool for not being honest about my true feelings"?

Whatever it was, I was ready for it. "What?" I asked innocently. I heard the rustling of pages. "This Marc Jacobs bag is two thousand dollars."

Oddly Unhappy for a Bride
on Her Wedding Day

♥

Nicole Hollander

In my wedding photos I look oddly pained. I look as if my wisdom teeth might be impacted, as if someone enormous had stepped on my toe. . . . I look as if my husband has just commented on my wedding outfit—the two-piece natural beige linen dress with a delicate embroidery pattern worked into the front panel in the same beige as the dress, bought the day before at that most subtle and impeccable store: Peck & Peck. . . . I look as if he has requested, in the calmest of voices, that I wear the top backwards so that the buttons are in the front and the embroidery in the back. He hates the embroidery.

Surely that comment was my cue to skip town, head for the hills or the first Greyhound bus for anywhere . . . maybe start a chain of pie shops. After all, the previous night, my mother had said, "It's not too late to change your mind."

But I knew that it was my destiny to be married, if only for a short time, to a man who felt that the width of noodles affected the taste of the soup and that I was deliberately choosing the wide kind to spoil the flavor.

I knew that being married would enable me to get away from my mother and earn an M.F.A. from Boston University, to be watching the Kennedy assassination on a television in a Harvard lounge at the same moment that the only reporter who knew both Kennedy and Oswald was in the same room.

I knew somewhere beyond my thinking brain, that someday my

-A WOMAN WHo HAS JUSt beeN tolD by HeR HusbANO to be thAt He HAtes the embroiDeRY oN HeR weDDiNÿ Dress.

-He HAS ASkeD iF SHe CoULD weAr the Dress bAckwArDs.

BACk oF Dress.

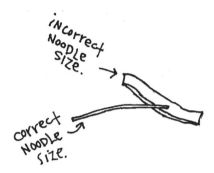

husband would say to me in a pleasant tone, "I like you very much, but I am teaching sociology to Radcliffe girls and they are swarming all over me and I would like to take one of them as my mistress . . . may I?" and I would have the chance to deliver the line that I will cherish with pleasure forever: "There's not enough in this marriage for one woman, let alone two."

Which led to my Mexican divorce, a fascinating and potentially dangerous experience in itself, allowing me to bring home some gorgeously decorated dissolution papers, bogus no doubt, and some real Mexican enchiladas to my delighted friends in Massachusetts.

Divorce papers, actual size.

When It Hit the Fan

❤

Hilary Schwartz

We had been seeing each other for a couple of months. He was intelligent, well read, and attractive. We enjoyed discussing books, politics, and cultural events.

On New Year's Eve I went over to his studio apartment. We were heading to a party at his friend's place later that night. We were kissing, and out of the corner of my eye I saw it sitting on the desk. It looked dark and shadowy. "Notice something?" he said with a twinkle in his eyes. I almost didn't believe it even as the words came out of my mouth, "Is that fake dog shit?" A huge guffaw erupted from deep in his throat. "Got you!" He laughed uproariously. "It's a great gag, huh? I'm bringing it to the party."

My heart beat faster as the realization crashed in my mind: I am in a relationship with a man who thinks fake dog crap is funny! And he's bringing it to a party! Dear God, what if he brought his pile of poo to a party with my friends? What if it escalated to hand buzzers and whoopee cushions?

I tried to fight it back, but my image of him was changing from cultured man to retarded frat boy. Just an hour before, I had envisioned a future of us sipping fine wine in museums. Now I saw a tomorrow of him spread out on the sofa in his underwear, watching NASCAR and burping Budweiser.

I tried to approach it rationally. I told him that I was more of a fan of verbal humor. He understood my appreciation of sarcasm and irony, and we discussed the merits of slapstick comedy. And all the while I'm thinking, I'm with a man who thinks fake dog crap is funny! We went to the New Year's gathering. A few people laughed at the faux feces, prompting me to think, I'm with a man who has friends who think fake dog crap is funny!

For the next two weeks, I processed the fake dog shit incident with friends and my therapist. Could this major difference between us ever be surmounted? But soon the shock faded, and I was able to see his good qualities again.

The relationship lasted a couple of years, on and off. But when it finally petered out, I had to admit that I had seen the end in that brown turd as clear as a crystal ball.

Boys Gone Wild

♡

Courtney S.

Man, he was good-lookin'. His wavy dark hair matched his worn leather jacket. He spoke with a commanding confidence while his eyes revealed no vulnerability. This modern-day James Dean was into little young me, the good girl who was toe-deep in adulthood. I was blinded.

When I learned this stunner was an intellectual, I referenced the classics and quoted recent studies. When I learned he sold marijuana for a living, I acted undaunted while inside I was aghast. I flaunted my coolness, my sexual openness. I pretended not to be impressed by his celebrity friends, bragged that I owned a vibrator, and channeled Gloria Steinem in intense political discussions. For weeks I visited the wild side with the good-lookin', leather-wearing, book-reading drug dealer!

That is, until he got a little too comfortable with me.

It was late when he called that last night. I told him he couldn't come over because I had an early flight. Turns out he was standing on my front porch. When I opened the door, he looked longingly into my eyes. It scared the shit out of me.

"I have to leave super-early to park my car at the airport. I have to go to sleep," I said, as nicely as possible. Obviously I was having trouble maintaining this bad girl lifestyle.

"Don't worry about it. I'll hire a car to take you."

Really? Well, all right.

He handed me the gift he'd been hiding behind his back: an original Beatles *Abbey Road* album. Damn. He's good.

He kissed me and told me he had a special night planned for us. After I promised to stay downstairs for ten minutes, he went upstairs to get ready.

My heart was racing. I was torn between "What the hell is going on here?" and "How sweet, this tough guy's doing something special . . . for me!"

Finally, I headed up the stairs.

Candles were lit. The lights were low. He was standing next to the bed wearing nothing but an orange button-down shirt and a smile.

Heart still racing, I smiled back. "Are you ready?" he asked.

"Okay," I replied in a quaky voice not appropriate for romantic situations.

He touched my cheek, turned around, and put his fists on the bed. "Where is it?" he asked, suddenly sounding angry.

"In the closet." I have no idea how I knew what he was talking about, but I did.

"Well, go get it," he said, as if I should always have it on my person.

In a daze, I walked over to the closet and pulled out my vibrator. I simply could not wrap my head around what he could possibly want with it. I'm not an idiot. I just couldn't grasp the idea that it involved me being anywhere near the situation.

When I returned, fake dick in hand, he was standing up straight again. He looked at me with great intensity before he dug his fists back into the mattress. He flipped up the tail of his shirt and with his bare ass high in the air he demanded, *"Give it to me."*

"What . . . ?" I sounded like a mouse. He wanted me to *use* the vibrator? On *him?* He didn't want to just see it? Or use it on me?

"Give it to me!"

"Uh . . . okay . . ."

I so very trepidatiously approached his butt. I raised, lowered, raised, lowered the vibrator. When I barely touched his rump I jumped as if I were the one being prodded.

"Come on!"

"I can't." I was almost in tears.

"Fine!" He grabbed the purple plastic penis out of my hand. He laid on his back and attempted to fuck himself. When that didn't work, he stood and squatted in the corner. *"Ow!"* he cried.

Not as easy as it looks, huh? I thought to myself.

After many failed attempts while I stood there with my eyes wide and mouth open, he ran to the bathroom in obvious discomfort.

Unfortunately this event wasn't enough to send my inexperienced body running for the singles bar.

With no time left to hire a car, he had to drive me to the airport. Oddly, he was not buckled over in humiliation. He seemed very, well, normal for a guy who had just attempted to take it in the rear in front of a captive audience. Was I being a prude? Am I so desperate that I'd blame this whole experience on my shortcomings? How is it possible that I still think he looks good in that jacket?

Since he'd taken me to my flight, I assumed he would be picking me up upon my return, what with my car not being at the airport because of his ass fetish.

"Can you pick me up at four o'clock tomorrow?" I asked nicely when he answered the phone.

"Uh . . . I don't know. I'm having a party tonight and I don't know how late it will go."

"I get in at four in the afternoon," I said. He must be high.

"Yeah, you never know."

I was getting pissed. "Listen, I need a ride, and you need to take care of it."

"Well, all right. Why don't you take a cab to my house, and I'll pay for it."

It would cost twice as much to take a cab to my house. I was broke. I took the fifty-dollar cab ride to his place. When I arrived at five o'clock, I had to knock for ten minutes with the meter running. When he answered the door half asleep, I finally saw him for what he was: a twenty-five-year-old wanker more unsure of himself than I'd ever be. I couldn't wait to get home.

"How much is it?" he asked.

"Fifty."

His eyes grew huge. "Fifty dollars? Wow." He scratched his head. "Can we split it?"

"Fine," I grumbled as I bit my lip.

He then proceeded to pull out a two-inch wad of twenty-dollar bills. He gave me one.

While he stood in the shade on his stoop, I grabbed my suitcases out of the cab. He grabbed his keys and walked ahead of me as I dragged said suitcases two blocks uphill to his truck. The ride home was not awkward, but some word that hasn't been penned yet that means awkward by a factor of twelve. Neither of us even bothered with a good-bye.

Having since grown a backbone and disposed of the vibrator, I look back at this as a pivotal learning experience. Now whenever a man asks me to have gay sex with him, I staunchly refuse.

Dark Bill

♡

Amy Turner

In a fit of first-month relationship giddiness he jumps out of bed one morning and goes to Gelson's for post-hump croissants. I am trying to be bon vivant cool, as if I always start my Tuesdays at nine with pastry, when in fact—unless I've gone to the gym and they are made out of a complete protein spelt flour—I run from croissants. I wait for him in bed, feeling lazy and sexy, like a Hilton sister. He returns with *The New York Times* and a mischievous twinkle in his big brown eyes.

"Got ya a little present, baby." He hands me a *Weekly World News*. "I didn't want you to know how much it was," he says, and I laugh at the kitschy gesture, examine the cover, and see that he is not kidding; he has actually crossed out the price with a pen. I don't say anything. On our first date he told me he couldn't be with a materialistic woman, but this is just bizarre. Before I met Bill, I thought that I just wanted something to climb all over and make me feel good, and I contemplated buying a jungle gym. But then I went to this party . . .

Standing rudderless in the din of celebrities and hangers-on at some newly anointed "edgy" screenwriter's house, I catch the strains of the Lucinda Williams song where she asks that her lover "don't cause me pain, just play me John Coltrane."

"I love this song," I say, and a man with dark hair flopping over dark eyes confirmed, "It is a very sexy song. She's crazy. I was at a bar in Nashville and the bartender almost tossed her 'cause she was so mean."

"You were at a bar in Nashville? Why?"

"I was there writing—"

At this point the neighbor who'd brought me to the party approaches and interrupts, "*Oh, my God!* Amy, have you met Bill? Bill, this is Amy. She's fabulous! She wrote the most beautiful book!"

"What do you do, Bill?" I ask.

"I'm a writer," he says. "Director."

"Interesting," says my hyperbolic neighbor. He tilts his head back, points at me, opens his mouth wide, like a Bette Davis muppet, and cries out, "This one is a genius!" Then he walks away. (The "book" the neighbor referred to is a collection of poems, of which there are ten hand-bound "limited editions" in circulation. Around my apartment.)

"What do you write?" says the dark Bill. I can't say, "I'm not sure, but my kitchen's covered with Post-it notes and it has the same effect as that scene with the air fresheners in the movie *Seven,*" so I say, "Oh . . . I'm working on a lot of different things right now. I'm uhm, an actor-writer." The writer title feels like a lie. I always identify myself as the thing I've most recently been paid for—unless it involves carrying a tray of food. I'd just come off a few months of being an actress. "Are ya any good?" he says.

"I don't know."

"That means you probably are." He smiles. And I smile, and it should've stopped right *fucking there* because the sky opened up, and an aurora borealis of neurosis exploded into one banner of light, spelling out: "I'm brilliant, I'm shit, love me!" And then he tells me about writing his script about Nashville and says, "The trick is to never do anything you don't want to do."

There were signs. Omens, actually. On our first date I was walking up to meet him at the movies, all first-date cute in pink skirt and virgin-whore mani-pedi (nail polish can be considered the modern-day female Rorschach test. Any woman with ballet slipper, baby pink on her fingers and wet, fire-engine, cherry-red on her toes is renting a condo in the virgin-whore complex). A car began honking at me, and I cringed until I saw it was Rick, my ex-boyfriend. I left Rick in Paris seven years ago with a combat boot toss at his head after he left for our four-week vacation in France with exactly one hundred dollars and no credit card.

Rick despised my "materialistic" tendencies. I did not want every dinner to be a home-cooked vegan feast, I liked the idea of a hotel or hostel and did not want to impose upon his French punk rock friends any more than need be. (If you've ever shared a bathroom with a French punk rocker, you will understand.)

It has come to my attention that if you're broke and you are my boyfriend, you complain about materialism a lot. You have a laundry list of excuses and voodoo dolls of corporate people who have screwed you out of deserved projects; on special occasions you take me to Thai restaurants with a C from the health department on the window, and you could be classified as clinically depressed except for the fact that you still have a voracious sex drive. At the time, this all seems romantic and charming, until I can't eat another bite of mee krob while you're blaming Wal-Mart for your lack of fame and fortune.

Seated in a café after the movie, Bill lays his life out for me like a D.A. making a closing argument. "I'm forty-three. I've been married. I'm not rich. I can't deal with women that are materialistic." I laugh, and ignore the materialistic reference. "You've been in L.A. too long," I say. I like him. He's funny and honest and handsome. So what if his shirt's threadbare and his shorts are missing the top button?

The next time we go out he invites me over to dinner at his friends' house and I am reminded of how our lives are in dramatically different places. He's forty-three, he's got friends with kids and outdoor grills. They're nice, but it is a social black hole, it feels like just yesterday I was vomiting in the Viper Room trying to find my four fake IDs and now I hear myself saying, "Love the salmon. What did you use for a marinade?"

Bill and I spent most of our time together late at night because I was waitressing. This was good, because we didn't spend money, and I worried about that. He kept going out of town for film festivals so the chemistry was thick, full of longing and reunions. He returned from one trip and had to head to a friend's engagement party, an event he invited me to. But I had learned to recognize the social black hole and declined, although I invited him over for a late-night visit afterward.

Fooling around immediately, kissing his fingers, nibbling the soft part between the thumb and index, I tasted a taste I'd recognize anywhere.

"Oh, my God," I say, my hand sandwich making me sick. "Did you do coke tonight?"

"Oh, God," he says.

"Oh, Jesus. You did coke tonight. Oh, my fucking God. Are you retarded? Why would you do coke tonight? Why would you do that when you know you're coming over here?"

"I just did a bump."

"That's lame. You're lame. Do you do coke all the time?"

"No. It was just friends, it was just there, I just did it, it was dumb."

"Yeah. It was. What do you mean you 'just did it'?" My face and nether regions puckered and I tried not to be judgmental.

"Honey, I'm sorry, it was stupid. I don't do drugs all the time."

"Whatever," I say. "I can't believe I just tasted it on you. I feel like a German shepherd."

"Next time I come over I'll bring you a 'don't pet me, I'm working' vest."

We developed a little joke about how we had yet to show the other any writing samples. We worried that if we hated each other's work we wouldn't be attracted to each other. He begged me for something, so I gave him some poems. A week later he came over, and said weakly, "I read your stuff. I liked it . . . but we need to talk about your use of the semicolon."

My use of the semicolon??? I turn over the Cliffs Notes to my soul and you give me blue pencil?

The next Sunday afternoon I invite Bill to join me on my walk.

(I'm a genius, I think, a free fun date.) Bill is a big guy, sexy-big, and he has cultivated the intellectual bohemian's smarmy repulsion for gyms or dietary concerns. He is a man with no workout regime and an unabashed love of bacon. Halfway through the walk he begins to complain. "You know, Amy, I've got a really bad knee." This is hard for me to deal with. My inner Texan football coach father is twanging, "It's a long way from your heart." Then Bill slows to a near crawl, puts his hands on his hips, and says, "Plus, I've got asthma."

"Walk it off, champ," I say.

He is sweating a lot. "How far are we going? You know, you're really in shape and I'm not, you can't just expect me to do this."

Then I snap. "I can't expect you to *walk?*"

"Not a million miles."

"It's not a million miles," I say. "It's two so far, maybe three. Tell me if you cannot walk. And then we'll call a doctor."

"You have no compassion. I'm going to take a taxi home."

We go on in silence for a while until we hit what I know is the halfway point, and he is fine. "Are you cool to get back home?" He won't look at me, but he nods. And on the way back he curses an actor on a billboard who declined an offer to be in his movie. I wonder why I have chosen an angry, sedentary guy. His wheeze grows in volume.

I begin to feel like I am married, only I didn't pick out the furniture and I have no idea what my husband does all day. He *hates* it when I come home and ask how his day was. I think this is because he hates to admit that he doesn't have much to say. He usually meets a friend for lunch, that's about all I ever get out of him.

Weeks slip by, and I try to drown out thoughts I deem superficial, thoughts such as, "Will he ever take me out to dinner and order a bottle of wine? Will he ever not watch TV in criminally unflattering volleyball shorts? Will I ever not worry about where he's finding the money for his rent and his bacon?"

I try and hide these thoughts because I love his bear-cave bed so much. I love the way I feel safe and real with him. I love the way when

I wake up he looks at me and says, "Good morning, gorgeous," and I actually feel gorgeous. I realize that he is my hiding place. And that is not okay.

Two weeks later I stop seeing Bill. I tell him I have to get more focused on what I need. He's confused and hurt. "Did I do something wrong?"

"No," I say. Because he didn't. He was just him.

After the first week I call him. He answers the phone sounding like Eeyore. "Everything's bad. My ex is suing me over the house, my screening was postponed 'cause I shot on the wrong film, and you're not around." I tell him I miss him. He asks if I can fit him into my life yet. "Use your words, Amy," he says.

"No, I can't fit you into my life." I hate him for making me say it, and I hate myself for saying it because it isn't true. The truth is I don't want to fit him into my life until he can be excited about his own. Sometimes I think I am Lucinda Williams and all I want is a lover who "don't cause me pain" and just "plays me John Coltrane," but it's not true. I want someone who is excited about working for his dreams. Bill turned me on when he said he never did anything he didn't want to do, because I dream of being that person so unaffected by the status quo, but I'm not.

I'm the girl who gets up over and over until they think I'm stupid or crazy or both. We get off the phone, and I kind of want to cry, but I hear that inner Texan football coach say, "Walk it off, kid, it's a long way from your heart." Maybe.

Video Killed the Love Story

♥

Aimee Cirucci

Tee and I didn't just fall in love, we plummeted. He would probably say we danced but only because his first words to me were an invitation to shag (in the Southern, not *Austin Powers*, sense). So we shagged into love. We met, realized we lived six hours apart, and the next weekend Tee was on my doorstep. Our third date was drunk with sober "I love you"s. Soon we were whizzing back and forth on I-95 like a couple of hurricanes, with the gale force winds of lust eclipsing our many differences, or at least making us think we could overcome them.

Tee was an avid video gamer and I a reader (books, magazines, food labels). I would fall asleep to the beep, beep, beep of his Sony X-Tendo and wake up early to read. His head on my stomach was perfect for balancing a book. He was ultraliberal, I was quietly conservative. He despised organized religion and I was a former Catholic schoolgirl. For our first Christmas I created a gift of all of his favorite indulgences: a nice dinner out, expensive whiskey, and Cuban cigars. He bought me a new TV.

To be honest, I didn't need a new TV; I didn't watch much TV and I didn't even have cable. The gift was made more awkward by the fact that Tee bought it right in front of me, paying for expedited shipping in an attempt to up the romance. On his first post-Christmas visit he sat entranced by his new toy. "Honey, did you see how the graphics look on this screen? Come check this out" was all I heard above the ringing and dinging of video games.

As my birthday approached so did my anticipation. I just knew Tee would get it right this time. I was so excited that I flew in to see him, wanting to be fresh and spry. As soon as I arrived I saw the two shiny wrapped packages addressed "To Honey" in black Sharpie ink. He insisted that I open them before we had dinner. I imagined books, perfume, theater tickets, jewelry. My head swirled with potential and my heart bubbled with love. As I shook the first box open I caught a glimpse of the new Super Mario Brothers glaring up at me. "These are video games for girls, hon, Super Mario and Rock Star and Zelda," Tee said. "We can play them together."

Splat! Our relationship fell flatter than the screen on my new TV. I didn't need high definition to see that we were both in love with the same person, and it wasn't me.

Oh, and for the record, the second package was video table tennis. I wouldn't play that even in real life.

... And the Matt Came Back

♥

Tina Dupuy

Back in the summer of '96 I was working at the needle exchange/harm reduction center on the Lower East Side. I was living in a squat on Avenue C. I was eighteen years old. I had pink dreadlocks and rings in my tongue, lip, nose, and nipples. I was what I now think of as a punk-hippie hybrid. Meaning, I plucked my eyebrows but didn't shave my armpits, I was a vegetarian who insisted on real leather Doc Martens, and I was totally for peace and love, save the occasional mosh pit.

Oh, the Clinton years!

The New York Needle Exchange at the time had two storefronts. I was an outreach worker for prostitutes, encouraging them to use clean needles and condoms. If anyone would ask why I was spending all my time with junkies and hookers, I would throw the Henry David Thoreau line at them: "Why aren't you?"

It was back in the good old days when it only took grunge going mainstream to make an entire generation "disillusioned."

This was when I met Matthew. He was a green-eyed twenty-three-year-old New York Film Academy acting student/artist who worked at a clothing store in the Village. I had rollerbladed past his store a couple of times. I remember at the time thinking that someone who had headshots was kind of exotic.

I had been in New York all summer. The place I stayed had no running water, so I would have to go over to a friend's house to bathe. Living in a squat is like camping without all the nature. You have to bring water up flights of stairs to flush the toilet. You have to find ways of getting electricity. You have to find creative tactics to keep you in and those that would like to steal your stuff out. It's not easy living rent-free. I was staying with a guy who went by the name of Tree. Not only was I sleeping with Tree, he was also servicing most of the women on our block. All with the same line: "It'll be fun and I won't bug you afterwards." It totally worked. All the time. He was a legend.

So Matthew's line, in the cutest Eastern Massachusetts/JFK accent, was: "My place in Brooklyn has a shower." And it totally worked.

I spent my last two days in New York in Matthew's apartment. We waltzed on his rooftop at midnight and took long walks along the brownstones. I told him he reminded me of Ricky Schroeder. He told me I reminded him of Tank Girl. I talked about my experiences at the Needle Exchange. He listened. I talked about what I thought about politics and history and movies and current events. And he listened. He was a great listener. And I love to talk.

I said, "I'm leaving tomorrow."

He said, "I love you tonight."

At least that's what I remember him saying. But I'll get to that in a minute.

I went back home to Oakland. We lost touch. I moved to Los Angeles, where on September 10, 2001, I ran into Matthew. Of course I would run into Matthew in L.A. He was an actor. He was an actor that had studied in New York.

Matthew was the first person that called me the next morning. "The U.S. is under terrorist attack."

Matthew and I spent the next week together, mostly. Watching the news, calling friends, and trying to figure out what this now meant.

I knew what I needed to do. I needed to be in a serious relationship with Matthew. At this point in my life I had never had a real boyfriend. And I knew that the attacks on America indicated that I should get one. I knew that it was meant to be. "If you love something, set it free" was that proverb. I set him free, here he was, the world was ending, better hook up—quick.

And then there I was. I was dating a boy who was an actor and an artist. I was in a relationship with a great anecdote that seemed like it was straight out of a Gabriel García Márquez novel, *Love in the Time of Terrorism*.

Now, I have what you could call a big personality. I like to talk. I like to voice my opinions. I like to tell stories and jokes. Sometimes I can be so comfortable being "myself" that I can be in the company of someone else and they can get ignored. Think of me as an only child with siblings. For some people this works really well. Because I am this self-amused I have completely missed glaring defects about people that I feel I am close to. For example: I had a friend in high school that I hung out with for a year before I ever noticed he had only one hand. Seriously.

"Everybody on the football team acts like they don't notice that I am different."

"Is it because you're black?"

"Black?! I have one hand!"

Stare.

In my defense he always had his non-hand in his pocket. But you can think of self-obsession as a sieve that will only let certain details through.

It was Thanksgiving and Matthew and I were going to spend it with his parents. And I was about to realize what I had gotten myself into. The catalyst to this was his mother. It seems Matthew's father was a genius physicist. He was like the Bob Dylan of Quantum Mechanics: the geek of a generation. The guy was brilliant. But his son, Matthew—my summer of '96 fling turned current boyfriend—was no Albert Einstein. He wasn't even a Taft-Hartley.

His mother was whipping up some Holiday Tofurkey in the kitchen when she dropped the bomb.

"When he was five he fell off a roof and landed on his head."

What I believe I said was, "Oh, that's terrible." And what I thought was—cringe—"Oh . . . that's *terrible*."

Mathew was a great listener and laughed at my jokes. But Mathew was, according to his mother, just slightly above mental retardation.

In the story of Sodom and Gomorrah, the innkeeper, Lot, and his two daughters are spared from this natural disaster of (of course) biblical proportions. And according to the Bible, Lot's daughters, thinking he is the only man left in the world, get him drunk and try to make themselves pregnant by him. Call it desperate times.

Now imagine the moment after that night the first time the daughters saw another town. And realized that in their haste they had made a cataclysmic mistake.

That's how it felt.

Much like Katie Holmes must have felt after the first time she said, "Gee, that Scientology stuff sounds pretty interesting."

How did this get past me?

Then it all made sense. Those aforementioned "pieces of artwork"? Collages. He cut out pictures from magazines and pasted them onto a canvas. If you can do it with rounded scissors, that's not art—that's arts and crafts.

I have had friends who asked why I was so mortified to date someone that was borderline retarded. To them I also use that Henry David Thoreau line: "Why aren't you?"

Now here's the moral dilemma: You cannot break up with someone just because they are borderline retarded. You can, however, easily trick them into breaking up with you.

Salad Bars with No Vegetables

♥

Wendy Hammers

For fourteen years, I was miserable, married, and fat.

As a comic, I did jokes about it: Weight Watchers! Can I help yous? Directions? Sure. We're located right next to the pancake house. Down from Burger King, across from Arby's. If you hit Bob's Big Boy, you've gone too far.

It worked. Sort of. I mean, my ass was the size of Delaware and my joy quotient was pretty low, but at least I got material out of it.

I would diet, lose weight, feel sexual, not have any place to go with those feelings, as my husband was depressed, unmedicated, and falling asleep in front of Sports Center. I didn't want to cheat on him, and I didn't know what to do with all the sexual energy I was feeling, so I would eat a little something, then a big something, then eat until I couldn't feel anything below my neck.

And it worked. The two or five or ten pounds that I had lost would reappear, my sexual cravings would disappear, and I'd be back where I started. I did this over and over and over and over for fourteen years.

Don't get the wrong idea. My marriage wasn't all bad. Oh, my God, no. We laughed. A lot. And traveled the country together, performing as a comedy team, a sort of postmodern, Jewish Lucy and Ricky, with our own little baby Ricky in tow.

But I was twenty-four when I met him and twenty-seven when we married, and well, that's just crazy shit. Someone should've just bitch-slapped me right there, like Cher did to Nick Cage in *Moonstruck*: "Snap out of it!"

Marrying before the age of thirty should probably be illegal, especially for a budding bad girl like me. I chose my husband because he seemed, at the time, like a good place to land. He felt like home. The relationship was grounding. Funny word, *grounding*. People always use it as a good thing, as in centered, stabilized. Of course, the flip side is when you're grounded, you can't get off the motherfucking ground. And I wanted so much to fly.

After all, it was only a short five years earlier, at nineteen, that I had lost my virginity to Juan Scarduzio, a half Italian, half Puerto Rican existential wrestler from Queens who was studying nursing at N.Y.U. Nice personality—although not the most ambitious guy in the world. I'd say, "Hi!" He'd say, "Wish I was." Eventually, I said good-bye to him and hello to Michael Riley, a newly sober comedian with absolutely no sense of humor. Then there was Franz Leitnerbrau, an Austrian film student who, as God is my witness, actually screamed "*Ja! Ja! Ja!*" when he was . . . yah, yah, yahing. And let's not forget the guy I slept with just because he looked like Jackson Browne. What can I tell you? He had flicky hair. I had no choice.

As soon as I tasted sex, I knew it was for me. I knew it that night in high school when James McFarlane and I were dry-humping for hours and hours on the mustard-colored, wall-to-wall shag in his parent's wood-paneled living room. I wanted more and I didn't even know exactly what more was. Just like raindrops on roses, sex had a few of my favorite things. It had passion, sensuality, theater, energy, joy, not to mention lips, tongues, hands, eyes. And aliveness.

Aliveness—that's what I was so hungry for—which brings me to

Judy, my spectacularly funny and vibrant friend of fifteen years. Judy was the funniest girl I ever met. Her résumé was impressive enough—founding member of the Groundlings, screenwriter of a movie called *Casual Sex*, writer on *Sex and the City*. But more than any of that, she was the kind of person that took her deepest darkest secrets, her neuroses and fears, and put them right into her act; she made you feel like she was nutty, but so were you, and if we were all a little nuts together, we were actually doing just fine.

Judy and I were like high school girls together, giggling on the phone, lying on the floors of our respective apartments, with our feet in the air, twirling phone cords—remember phone cords? We would gossip for hours and hours, looking like we were doing a production of *Bye Bye Birdie*, only to have Judy sign off with her signature, "Gotta run, doll. Call me every five minutes."

As stand-up comics, we toured together. During Madonna's "Blond Ambition" tour, we did what we called our "No Ambition" tour—eleven hell gigs in fourteen nights: Montana, Colorado, Wyoming, and Utah. Lots of salad bars with no vegetables, just fruit cocktail with marshmallows; Jell-O with stuff. Like I said—hell gigs, but heaven with Judy. She was, quite simply, very alive. More than most.

Until she died. Melanoma. Skin cancer. In the spring of '02. She was only forty-four and a newlywed and had been married for nine months to an incredible man that she had met three years earlier on J Date. Almost immediately, they fell deeply, deeply in love.

They had three years together, three amazing ones, which, for my money, are a helluva lot better than thirty not-so-hot ones. But the defining moment—the aha, the turning point (call it what you like)—came when sitting shiva for Judy. Her husband, Rick, said the reason she had waited so long to marry was because she didn't want to settle.

Settle.

The word floated out of his mouth and lodged itself in my brain. That's what I had done. I had settled. What was I doing here, in my dead marriage? Who was I being here? And how was I to get out of here? There I was sitting on a couch, there to support my friend's newlywed and newly widowed husband, and all I could think was that I had settled in my marriage. I felt like a jerk, self-centered and inappropriate. But I knew I had to get out, or I would die. Not like my precious friend, in the hospital with tubes and oxygen and in a coma, but rather, a different kind of dead. The walking dead. And like my friend, I couldn't breathe. I was suffocating, and I was goin' down.

In that defining moment, I looked across the couch at my husband. I really looked. I did not let myself turn away, which would have been easy to do. I saw a man I'd known, in every sense of the word, for seventeen years, and he was a stranger. I knew and saw all of that. I had loved him. But I knew I was done. That we were done. I just knew. Sometimes you know, but you don't want to know what you know. For years I looked away. This time, finally, I didn't.

Smitten No More

♥

Kerry Monaghan

In March 2006, I was living in Boston and went to see Ted Leo and the Pharmacists with friends at the Paradise Rock Club. It was a heady time—I was about to quit my job and backpack in Europe for a few months before moving to New York City.

After the show we got pizza across the street and played some Modest Mouse on the jukebox. There was a guy sitting by himself at the next table. My uninhibited little hand waved. He waved back with a shy smile. His name was Scott, and we started talking about the concert (he had seen Rob Livingston at the venue next door) and his plans to move to Maui to drive a taxi. I asked when his birthday was and he said, "Today." Scott pulled up a chair at our table.

The next morning, I had an e-mail: "MySpace Friend Request! Scott would like to be added as one of your friends." I told my friends that the "pizza boy" had tracked me down after getting home to Providence at 3:39 A.M., but I was more happy than creeped out.

We exchanged some flirty e-mails, he asked if I had a boyfriend (no) and said he wanted to hang out before he moved to Hawaii in a week. My shyness kicked in and I brushed him off. Scott left for Hawaii, and I wrote him a good-bye haiku, which was a coincidence because he was moving to a town called Haiku. We stayed in touch.

Yes, I stayed in touch with this kid who went to concerts by himself on his birthday, stalked me on the "intarwebs," and moved to Maui to drive a cab.

While he was gone, I read in Scott's blog about his experiences in Maui: trouble securing a driver's license from the DMV, spearfishing, climbing volcanoes, cooking hamburgers, sleeping on a friend's couch, feeling homesick. He posted pictures of sunsets and grazing cows and new friends and the mustache he grew for a bet. I liked his eye for photography, his sense of humor, his clever writing.

We talked over Instant Messenger when Scott was up late in Hawaii and I was waking up in Boston. Who knows what we chatted about? All I know is that he made me laugh and smile, and understood me better than some of my closest friends. He was no longer "pizza boy," but a friend that I cared about.

Just before I quit my job and took a one-way flight to Rome, I started dating a guy from Boston. (Whoops.) Despite this, I kept in contact with Scott throughout my two months of traveling.

Scott returned from Hawaii around the same time I got back from Ireland. We both moved in with our parents while looking for jobs. We updated each other on job prospects and he showed me his résumé, which listed "octopi, robots, and post-apocalyptic movies" as interests. He teased that when he was having a bad hair day, he would think of me and feel better. We became insomniacs, since we had no jobs to wake up for, and chatted late into the night. He always signed off with "sleep sweet, Kerry."

Meanwhile, my boyfriend and I were fighting. When we took a break, I drove to Boston to cry on my best friend's shoulder. This was the first of many times that I "swung by" Providence to see Scott.

This was a big deal: it was eight months after our first meeting. Scott and I met outside Tealuxe in Providence. Awkward hug. He bought me tea. My hands were shaking. I told him he was tall. What I meant was: you are taller than the Scott that has existed in my head for the past eight months. And you have a lisp. It's not a bad lisp. But now I have to superimpose a tall, lisping Scott over the Scott that I conjured up from your MySpace page. On top of that, your shoes are superglued together. The Scott I had been crushing on all this time is shorter and less scrawny and cockier and has perfect elocution and intact footwear.

My head was spinning.

Tealuxe was crowded so we took a walk. It was drizzling. Scott did most of the talking; I contributed nervous giggles and worried that my outfit was all wrong. He talked about bread crust—he needs the little air pockets in slices of bread to be lined up, and the crust cut with precision. He also talked about his parents and older brothers and Providence and his new apartment and socks and how he missed spearfishing. Then it was time to go, and we hugged and promised to see each other soon. He hugged me again, squeezing hard.

I drove home and tried to sort it all out. The Scott I had created in my mind dissolved, and was replaced with the real-life tea-drinking crust-discussing mildly lisping guy. I was smitten.

Meanwhile, I had a failing relationship to go home to. My boyfriend and I broke up within a few weeks. I moved to New York City, started a stressful job, and had a devastating breakup one month before Christmas. It was a trifecta of darkness and depression at the loneliest time of the year. My only shimmer of hope was that Scott would rejoice to learn that I was single and soften these blows.

No such luck. He didn't scoop me up now that I was available, which was like experiencing two breakups at the same time. We still talked, but it wasn't enough—I wanted to be with him. When Scott introduced me to his best friend in Brooklyn, it felt like a setup, but when I got home that night I called him right away. Scott said, "So, I take it you're not in love with Alex? Good."

Scott sent Alex and me an e-mail about coming to New York for New Year's Eve. He wanted to see *Evil Dead: The Musical,* and sit in the splatter zone where you get hit with fake blood. That was not my thing at all, but no matter, I was thrilled. Then Scott flaked out, without ever giving a reason.

The months went by, and I pulled my life together. Spring sprung. Trees grew in Brooklyn. I sent Scott an e-mail on his birthday, the anniversary of when we met. Scott told me he had driven past the Paradise the night before, saw that Rob Livingston was playing there again, and told a friend all about me. We made plans for me to come to Providence, and that weekend I met Scott's friends, we played Ping-Pong, watched *The Incredibles,* held hands, had our first kiss.

That Sunday, Scott flew to Canada for his job, so I made excuses when I didn't hear from him for a few days. No phone calls, no e-mails, no nothing. Then we entered a holding pattern where he popped in and out of my life every week or so. The highs of hearing from him were tempered by the lows of *waiting* to hear from him. He hated his job and I told him he deserved better, and he immediately started interviewing and got a better job. That was the thing—we influenced each other way out of proportion to how well we knew each other.

We saw each other for the fourth time when I was up in Boston that summer for a party. My friends knew about Scott, and how he could make or break my mood, so they didn't want me to invite him. They were trying to protect me, but the addict needed her fix. I called him and he joined us for the party. When it was time for him to get back to Providence, I walked him to his car and we made out like teenagers.

I thought for sure he would call, or come visit, or at least regularly e-mail me after that weekend. No. He maintained the holding pattern. Didn't call for two weeks, then called from the airport before flying to Brazil on a mission trip. Melt my heart. How can you stay mad at someone who is going to help the kiddies? I could not. I was the kitten and his attention was the ball of yarn dangling before me.

Over Labor Day weekend, I "swung by" on my way to Cape Cod. We went to a karaoke bar and I slow danced with his friend Chris to "Cruisin'." I couldn't believe it when I saw Scott shoot Chris a look of death while we danced together. He, who had kept me at arm's length all these months, was jealous? I was charmed.

After that weekend I asked Scott to come to my sister's wedding. He was the perfect date: he gave me pep talks before my toast, he wasn't clingy when I had to do bridesmaid stuff, and we danced the whole night. The photographer assumed we were a couple and when he snapped a picture said, "You two might be next!"

My parents, even more enamored than I was, asked me why Scott wasn't my boyfriend, and I explained that he wouldn't call for two weeks after the wedding. Sad, but true. The next time I heard from him was when I received an invitation to his Christmas party in Providence.

When I e-mailed him to ask if he really wanted me to come, he wrote back, "It's kind of a long drive, isn't it?"

Boom.

That was it. After a year and a half of being nudged away, I had been shoved to the ground. The King of Mixed Messages invited me, but didn't want me to come. I was smitten no more. I remembered the disappointment of Scott flaking out on *Evil Dead: The Musical* a year before, and realized what a fool I had been to stay on this roller coaster.

The problem was, Scott was everywhere I turned. So I deleted him from MySpace, Facebook, Last.fm, Gmail, and my phone. In this hyperconnected age, there is no graceful way to end relationships that are hurting you. But technology can help.

His reaction? Radio silence.

I'm a little sad, and a lot relieved.

Not to mention, I met this cute guy last night at Whole Foods.

Fantasy Ain't Reality

❤

Rachael Parenta

We Americans like to say the third time is a charm. Unfortunately, for Ben and me two-and-a-half times isn't so charmed and just doesn't cut it.

Ben and I had made two attempts at dating each other. We failed. After that we tried varying forms of relationships from immaturely ignoring each other to basic civility to awkward friendship. You see, I had shat where I ate, which is always a good idea—you should shit where you eat, this way you don't waste anything. Ben and I work in the same industry, so his riding off into the sunset never to be dealt with again wasn't possible. Oopsy.

Two years went by and one drink led to another, which led to sex. So we were having sex once or twice a week, but we weren't "together" (which is how I get the half attempt in my calculation above). Because of the shit-eating situation during this time we found ourselves at the same East Village bar on the same night. With a few drinks swimming in both of us, and our sexual relationship already reestablished, we began the negotiations of who would get to host the end of the evening. Ben said we had to go back to his apartment because he had some appointment in the morning—which I really didn't believe—and he'd never make it if we went back to my place in Brooklyn. I couldn't go back to his place because I had to work my day job in the morning, which required me to dress business professional. The problem is I don't usually dress the same for an East Village bar where the bartender goes by the name Mangina as I do for a corporate law office. I couldn't borrow something from his closet: He's twice my size, and I don't think he owns a suit—male or female.

In true us fashion we spent probably an hour arguing about where we should go and if not that night then later in the week sometime. The more we debated the fewer people remained in the bar. Exasperated and horny, he suggested we give the bathroom a try. I thought to myself, Yeah! Fuck, yeah! I'm a sexually adventurous woman and now I can prove it! Look at me, Mom, I'm a New York City woman! I'm an adult and I'm going to have sex in the bathroom of a bar. I rock. I thought this was a great opportunity and I should seize the moment. The bathrooms at this East Village bar were logistically ideal for a first-time public sex act. The thick wooden doors travel from the ceiling to the floor, leaving no gap for anyone to peer in. To make matters better, the bathrooms were single-stall and locked.

It turns out my imagination is hotter than reality. It was kind of gross in there. If there was ever a time to use a condom, it was in the bathroom of this bar. There was toilet paper strewn about, parts of the floor were wet, and there was a pervasive dampness. I'm not much of a skirt wearer but I wished I had been wearing one so I wouldn't have had to balance my pants being lowered enough to have sex but not too low that they touch the floor. In hindsight I realize I could have taken them off and slung them over my shoulder; genius never strikes at the right time.

So we get to it. He lifts me up. That doesn't really work because he can't keep me up, or rather he sort of can but he has to lean back, and it's awkward. I'm not big, people. I'm like five foot one and weigh one hundred and five pounds, and he's more than five foot ten and more than one hundred and five pounds. I thought he should be able to hold me up, especially if I'm braced against the wall, but he can't. No big deal. I mean, I'm having sex in a bathroom. I'm still winning. Undeterred, I suggest he sit on the toilet. (I wouldn't find out until the next day, after I sent a mass e-mail to friends asking for advice, that the best position for public bathroom sex is standing—though with our height difference and his lack of athleticism, I think that still would have been a challenge.)

I suggest we move to him sitting on the toilet and me sitting on top of him (so to speak). An enthusiastic lover of sitting, he quickly agrees. We're just getting to it again and he says, "I should fart right now," or something like that. He mentioned himself and the act of passing gas—describing the gas-passing as a fart. I responded sardonically, "Oh, that's hot." It seems Ben never got the memo that talking dirty doesn't mean scatological. I'm thinking, Jesus Christ! It's gross enough in here without your ridiculous comments. Focus! A minute went by and I heard a sound—like a grade-school child playing the tuba for the first time—reverberate out of the porcelain, bounce off the right wall to the left wall back to the right wall, and then rattle in my head. I felt humiliated, which is ridiculous. I wasn't the one who farted. But I chose to have sex with him. . . .

That was the moment I knew we didn't work in any capacity. Not as friends, not as romantic partners, and definitely not as a couple engaging in bathroom sex.

That bar is gone now, but I'll always have that memory . . . and now so will you.

Starter Marriage

♥

Michele Gendelman

Some women know their marriage is over on the honeymoon. Others, after they discover that the man they married is a bigger baby than the one they just gave birth to. Still others, after they open their husband's briefcase looking for the checkbook and find a light-blue, lace-trimmed Felina satin thong that isn't theirs—or worse yet, that belongs *to* their husband.

I knew my marriage was over after the rehearsal dinner. It just took me two years to realize it.

For some time I'd had a casual social acquaintance with a man I'll call J., a twenty-five-year-old ponytailed postgraduate student living in my hometown of Washington, D.C. Then one evening J. and I ran into each other at a party and it was love at second sight. He was bright, cocky, and supportive, a bus-and-truck Richard Dreyfuss with a Ph.D. We became engaged six months later.

Our wedding was set for early September, several weeks before I was to begin graduate school in Los Angeles. After the brief rehearsal the evening before, J. and I took some friends out to a Greek restaurant. The food was so-so but the bouzouki band was loud and the belly dancers enthusiastic. When our waiter learned of our impending nuptials he made sure the sloe-eyed houris lost no time undulating toward my delighted fiancé.

As we left the restaurant later that night, shouts followed us outside onto the street. J. told me to pay no attention and keep walking. It was our waiter, yelling that J. had not tipped him. J. helped me into my car, assuring me that he'd indeed left a gratuity, and a handsome one. It was an old ploy: let's embarrass the groom in front of the bride and squeeze a bigger tip out of him. " 'Sh'right," I said, through a haze of retsina and ouzo. "You can't trusht thezhe people. Member wha they did to Troy."

This being the late seventies, and me being a feminist, I'd decided to buck Jewish tradition and be the one to break the glass at the end of the wedding ceremony. Earlier that week, in the midst of those million last-minute details that precede all weddings, I'd given J. five dollars to buy a single wine goblet at the local department store, something delicate and thin that would shatter easily beneath my high heel.

The next morning, after we exchanged our vows before assembled family and friends, the best man placed the glass before me, wrapped in a linen napkin. I raised my foot. "One small step for woman, one giant leap for Jewish womanki—" There was a thud as my heel hit what felt like a rock; pain shot up my leg and I windmilled backward into my eighty-two-year-old grandmother. J. saved the day with his double-E-wide Earth Shoe. "Mazel tov!"

As everyone headed off to the reception I knelt down and discovered it wasn't a crystal wineglass but a grocery-store jelly jar, half an inch thick. I couldn't have broken it with a sledgehammer. J. shrugged. The jar cost thirty-nine cents, leaving four dollars and fifty-three cents after tax; why waste money? I chose not to question his decision and limped off to join our guests.

I did, however, confront him several days later during our cross-country journey to California, when he refused to "let" me buy a four-dollar bottle of Revlon Moon Drops moisturizer in an Iowa City drugstore. I held my temper until we got outside, then pointed out that this was *my* money, too. I'd spent two years at a job I loathed, saving for tuition and living expenses; I didn't have wealthy parents picking up the tab for grad school as he'd had. When he pronounced me an "irresponsible spendthrift," I took the car and drove off, leaving him somewhere between the University of Iowa and a cornfield, which pretty much describes all of Iowa City. After driving around for ten minutes I returned and apologized. He asked if I had any idea how much money I'd wasted, what with regular going for 62.9 cents a gallon.

Not long after we settled in L.A., J.'s boss took us out to dinner at a chichi place in Beverly Hills. At the end of a pleasant evening, we, the boss, and his wife went down to the parking garage, where J. graciously insisted that the valet bring the boss's car first. We waved good-bye as they drove off, the good food and fine wine suffusing us with warmth and optimism. Then the valet brought our car around. No sooner had he shut my door than J. floored it and sped out of the parking structure, tires squealing like pigs in an abattoir, leaving the valet to shake an empty fist at us. J. hadn't wanted to ruin a "perfect" free evening by having to tip fifty cents.

The following year I gave birth to a beautiful blue-eyed boy. My life became a mad race from apartment to day-care to campus and back again, with a little guy who liked to eat in tow. When a friend told me microwave ovens were ideal for heating baby food, I comparison shopped and bought one for ninety-nine dollars and ninety-nine cents, well within our budget. J. hit the roof. A hundred dollars to heat something in seconds when bottles and jars could be warmed on the stovetop in five minutes and teach the child patience besides?! He grabbed the receipt, shoved the oven back in its box, and returned it to the store.

The next week he took a thousand dollars from our joint savings (without consulting me) and bought himself a motorcycle.

Not long after that I took three hundred dollars from our joint savings (without consulting him) and bought myself a divorce.

In every marriage the purse strings and the heart strings are closely intertwined. Stingy with money; stingy with emotion. A man who's cheap prides himself on his ability to get something for nothing; and that, alas, includes you and your love.

Cuckoo for Cocoa Puffs

❤

Dorit Simone K. F.

D azbog Branislav was my first. He was interesting. I'd say cozy with potential. But Dazbog was unique in that he was a Queens, New York–born, blue-eyed, tall, boyish man, with dimpled cheeks and a thick heavy-duty blond Jewfro on top of his head. Not only that but he was physically huge. So, I felt safe in his realm. I will never forget the feeling of his 260-pound, six-foot-four body on top of my nineteen-year-old 123-pound virgin innocence. Lying in bed, directly on top of me, giggling, he grabbed onto each one of my legs. I felt like a chicken about to be roasted on his Sunnyside, Queens, lawn. Suddenly, animal cruelty had a whole new meaning and in that bleak moment I contemplated becoming a vegetarian. Dazbog went quickly from making me feel safe to making me want to run. He dug his face into my neck and then crawled his tongue up to the back of my ear. I remember thinking that he might have been a puppy in a former life because he went on to licking my earlobe like he was trying to clean it. Or maybe he had OCD and was counting each lick. I couldn't help but start to count myself . . . it felt like counting sheep. In fact, I almost fell asleep but he began to mumble a phrase. Since his parents are Russian he sounded like a mix between Mikhail Gorbachev and Rudy Giuliani (swear to God). I kept thinking, Is he reciting some biblical blessing—koshering the experience? (FYI—when kosher chickens are slaughtered, each one is blessed individually.)

It was hard to get his attention. So after repeated attempts, I kicked him in the ass and screamed, "*Dazbog, what are you saying?*" He paused and became still. It was silent. He cautiously leaned into my ear and very breathy, in a Queens, New York, and Russian accent said, "I'm cuckoo for Cocoa Puffs." And that was it. *Cuckoo for Cocoa Puffs?* I guess it was one of the few American phrases that he could muster up at the height of passion. Or maybe he was just hungry. Whatever the deal was, it didn't matter. The flash of my life hit. The channels of my this-is-not-going-to-work-out relationship radar opened, but not wide enough. The words came to me, but only in a whisper, "Get out! Run! This is not for me. . . ."

About a week later he moved out to Vegas to try acting. To make extra money he worked for an escort service. He swore he was just "escorting" old lonely women to high-profile events: "Just dinner, I promise," he said. He came back to New York five weeks later and stopped by my apartment the next day. His dick was peeling as if he had a sunburn. He told me that he was horny while in Vegas. Sitting at home by himself thinking of me, he looked around the room and couldn't find anything greasy, so he used the Clorox to jerk off. He did this until his penis burned and the skin on his balls started to peel. How nice of him to have been thinking of me. That was when I knew for sure. The game was over. The whisper turned into a loud voice, "*Get out, run,* this is not for me . . . this guy is not for me . . . *whatever* this is, is not for me."

Son of a Preacher Man

♥

Melinda Culea

H e was tall with blond curls, funny, and a great kisser. Well, suffice it to say that I had tried to enjoy the sharing of lip intimacy with others, but nothing came close to the journey I experienced with this man's mouth. This was the real thing.

We met in the autumn, Joni Mitchell's lustrous crooning haunted the airwaves and our antiwar sentiments were the communion we expressed in tattered jeans, moccasins, and peace symbols. Not rising for the Pledge of Allegiance was our stance against all that our grandparents had built. Discussing the *New Yorker* cartoons was the sole curriculum for our creative writing course. *The Last Temptation of Christ* was our tattered companion as we lay drenched in each other and Erik Satie. Did I mention he was the son of a preacher man?

The first time I laid eyes on him was at a sunrise prayer meeting he led in the stained-glass chapel. I was a guest of my newfound friend, who had the most luxurious long locks and eyelashes. She was the brain in our honors English class and I was fascinated with everything about her. She danced as if she were on acid and the eye shadow kit she pulled out nine times a day was the best combination of four frosted colors you have ever seen. She was hardly vain, having attended a small private religious school. I believe she was just breaking out in her new life as one of five thousand public school attendees. She was cool.

She invited me to hear her speak at her youth group. They served powdered sugar donuts and that was enough for me. I listened to her. I stared at him. She was good. He was glorious. His best friend played the organ. I was given a tour behind the enormous pipes in the enormous sanctuary. I have always loved churches and this was one to behold. Both he and his father looked good in robes. Clerical robes I mean.

He called me the next day for a date on Friday. We saw *Z* and my mind was reeling when he kissed me goodnight. Saturday he came to a football game where I was cheering and got permission to drive me home. We stopped in the forest preserve for a little lotta necking. And by Sunday morning service he could have my soul. Big time. The reverend preacher father-of-my-new-boyfriend was also the leading man in the fight against dress codes at school. He was well known as a rebel and all-around hip guy. He organized trips to join Jesse Jackson in Operation Breadbasket rallies in Chicago. He gave great inspiring sermons and was tall, blond, and handsome himself. My understanding of the wrongness of the Vietnam War evolved from attending prayer services for the soldiers and heavy discussions after watching film documentaries.

In the house the church provided for this fine minister, his wife, and his four kids, Dionne Warwick sang Bacharach music on every Saturday afternoon. No one was allowed to knock on the preacher's bedroom door. He and his wife were taking naps that surely left her looking glowing and refreshed. One of the older sisters was a Playboy bunny at a summer resort to earn money for college. This family of people had me so hooked. Did I mention my own father was warring with his brother and having serious business problems to boot?

Times were passionate. My earlier commitments had me still attending basketball games as the cheerleading captain to an audience of thousands. But not before the quick tryst in his unheated car, mitten on hand, hand on him, and shooting stains left on my golden uniform panties. That later turned oddly to blue when washed. Thereafter when we walked in the freezing cold wind after another victory game, I clenched my skirt bottom for fear of exposure. And of course, cartwheels were always a concern. His old girlfriend I often spied in the crowds and I wondered at the colors on her underwear. My brother said she was loose.

I thought I was loose. I couldn't please enough. We drove downtown to catch *Love Story* and I could not stop crying. He said I looked just like her. Which I did, sort of, and he gave me a hat like she wore. I began flaring my nostrils.

As the silent snowy evenings turned to melting spring, he was busy planning for college. I was busy planning an early graduation, as I was two years younger than he was. I needed night school and summer school and advanced testing. The best-case scenario still left me one year behind. The prom was ever looming. My chest had refused to grow and the pretty halter-top dress I had chosen left no room for padding. Suddenly the similarities to Ali McGraw seemed unfortunate. And though the war raged, my thoughts were increasingly on my own little world. In church I prayed that the next year would fly by.

The motorcycle he bought to take a trip cross-country left a big infected burn on my leg. The visits to the doctor came amid my summer school classes. His letters grew scarcer and so did my energy. I got strep and then mono. He decided to travel north to his family's cabin in Wisconsin. I stayed home in bed. Finally, in August I ventured up for a visit. He was distant. I was still tired. We rode on his cycle along the back roads. He lingered a little too long in front of one house where he said he met a family who sang in the church he attended up there. The girl played the xylophone and was going to the same university he was!

By the fall, I was thrilled to know I had just one year left. I wore one of his old shirts nearly every day. I liked my classes and couldn't wait to visit him at college. The phone calls weren't too frequent or too great. Finally, his sister and I drove up for the visit. We were in the very same car that he and I had shared so many romantic moments together. My passion was primed. Acres of cornfields flew by as we listened to more Motown than you knew existed. She was very cool and I had borrowed one of her outfits, as I loved how she dressed. Again, she was part of that perfect family.

When we arrived he was okay. He seemed preoccupied. I figured it was being away. Anyway, the whole weekend felt weird and I increasingly relied on his sister for communication. We drove back singing "Just My Imagination."

Next Saturday, he was coming home to visit! It was our anniversary and his birthday and the day I had to take college exams. So, that Friday night when he surprised me by coming home early, I handed him a fabulously fuzzy teddy bear and a cashmere sweater— to keep him feeling loved and cozy. My hug felt unreciprocated.

"I'm breaking up with you. There's someone else."

"You met her at college?"

"Well, she goes to my college, but we met this summer."

And so on and so forth. We kept talking until midnight, I had to get up early. So, he left. Of course, it didn't matter, I did not sleep. He met me after the most important test of my life. And we walked and talked again for hours. Finally when I could no longer move as my eyes were so swollen from the gallons of tears that would not end, I sat down on the curb. I remember swearing off all of my faith in anything godly—him, his father, his church. This pain was so deep in me I wanted to stop breathing. But I didn't get a chance because right then a big old black bird, we call them crows, came along and pooped on top of my head.

It was that moment . . .

CONTINUED ...

Open Season

♡

Katherine Ruppe

My friend Alyson always told me geeky guys were more interesting. I took her words to heart a few years ago, resolving to add more conventional types (okay, nerds) into my dating mix. Up until then my network consisted solely of adventurous, charming, yet fatally flawed boy-men, one of whom had recently left me stranded at dusk with a flat tire while mountain biking down a ravine known to be frequented by mountain lions. Geeks could only be an improvement, and this normally thrill-seeking screenwriter was looking to find herself one.

So with Alyson's refrain in mind I met the Engineer. He was good-looking in a serious, Clark Kent way, if Clark Kent was blond with even bluer eyes. Sure he was a brainiac with a couple of graduate degrees and a military-industrial complex job, but he also indulged in Red Bull and Jägermeister, was an athlete, and had a playful side. Maybe I could have my Clark Kent and a spicier Superman, too.

Our first date was initially strained. Engineers never seem to speak without first making complex internal computations. Luckily, after a few of his signature cocktails he loosened up and we had a great talk about spiritualism, near death experiences, and flying (he owned a plane—very hot). I melted a little when he held my hand and told me I was more beautiful than he remembered, and was tickled when he spoke eagerly of future dates we would take. His goodnight kiss was a little mechanical (like him?), but I still got girlish goose bumps. I went to sleep that night feeling unexpectedly tingly.

Two weeks later we had our second date in Las Vegas, where he was temporarily working. My love of adventure had won over my true need for caution in the romance department; besides, I felt like we had made a real *connection*. I'd like to say Vegas was all high-rolling romance, but I'd be fibbing. We were simply two people growing more and more in lust in a bland business motel complete with free (!) happy hour beer and hot wings. After two days he flew me in his speedy single-engine back to L.A. under a blanket of cotton candy clouds. His sexy pilot's voice drove me crazy while his explanations of wing load put me to sleep. Is that what life with Superman was all about?

Back in L.A., visions of boyfriendship danced through my head. The Engineer seemed to be on a different flight plan. It took him more than a week to call me, leading me to question whether Vegas had just been a mirage, and I don't mean the hotel. By our next date, however, our *connection* had returned so strongly that I set aside my dismay and invited him to a Moby concert.

Twenty-four hours later I was lazing on my couch when the Engineer phoned. I thought, How nice, he's calling two nights in a row. He must really like me. Instead he sent my stomach into a neat back flip with the words: "There's something we need to talk about." I braced myself.

Him: "So, I'm sure you must realize I date other women."

Me (breezy): "Uh, sure." (Although I can't imagine why you'd want to.)

Him: "But there's one woman I'm more serious about than the others."

Me: "Oh?"

Him: "Her name is [the Schoolteacher]. We've been going out for a year and a half."

Me: "You have a girlfriend?"

Him: "She's just someone I see more regularly than the others."

Me: "You have a *girlfriend*."

Call me naïve; I have this tendency to believe that men who are dating me are actually *available*. But wait. The Engineer was available . . . they have an open relationship. He went on: "What may seem even weirder . . . she wants us all to have dinner before the Moby concert this weekend." I felt an out-of-body experience coming on. Strange, he hadn't advertised this fabulous Two-for-One Deal when we started dating.

"Why does she want to meet me?" my out-of-body voice inquired.

"I don't know," he replied, "she likes to meet some of the girls I see. . . . Circumstances aside, you two could probably be friends because you're both smart and she also likes hiking and biking." So now he was setting me up with his girlfriend. How thoughtful. One word kept going through my head: Freaks!

What can I say? I may be a city girl, but I'm small town at heart. I pressed him again on why she wanted to meet me, suspecting they wanted a threesome, although this was never brought up. The Engineer reasoned she meets his "friends" when she feels threatened by them. She also has a rule: he can't date her friends. So I guess by becoming friends with me it would mean he could no longer date me. Who was this Jezebel? She was brilliant!

I flatly told him I had no interest in meeting his ball and chain and hung up. Looked like I'd be finding a new date for Moby. As I poured myself a bucket of wine, I mourned the passing of the Engineer as a potential boyfriend. Why couldn't men surprise me with roses or trips to Paris instead of requests like "My girlfriend wants to meet you"? Had dashing off to Vegas made me seem like such a fun-lovin' gal that I'd want to be the third wheel in someone else's relationship? So much for going for nerdy guys. They were *interesting,* all right.

After my brief whine session, the Steven Spielberg (Soderbergh?) in me became intrigued. Maybe there was a screenplay in this. I also got angry. While I blamed the Engineer for his dishonesty, I was peeved that his girlfriend seemed to be pulling all the strings. I didn't like being manipulated. So I decided to fight back. Although I preferred to call it research.

I e-mailed the Engineer that I'd meet his girlfriend after all. He replied he'd check with her and closed with: "I hope this still means we're on for the concert!" I didn't reveal that cows would turn blue before I'd be taking him to Moby. Instead, my screenwriter's eye envisioned a scenario for our upcoming date: We'd meet in a romantic restaurant, the Engineer flanked by his two main squeezes, his computer brain whirring uncomfortably as she and I chat like new best friends. Over dessert, I'd zing them with the hypocrisy of their not-so-open open relationship. I'd inform them that I like to be the star of my own romantic dramas, thank you very much. Then I'd flounce off, leaving them dazed and contrite in my defiant wake. To prepare for my role, I even studied up on open relationships and their combative cousins, swinging and polyamory. The great thing about writing was that I could explore brave new worlds without actually getting my hands dirty. Or so I thought.

Like all great summits, our meeting became an on again/off again affair as a tiff developed between the Schoolteacher and the Engineer. I don't want to sound vain, but I think it was about me. I seized the opportunity to quiz him by phone about their relationship. "What are the rules?" He wasn't sure, they had changed so many times, but one rule was he had to tell the Schoolteacher in advance when he was going out with someone else and then they'd discuss it afterward. *Ick!* I always wanted to be talked about, but not like that. He pointed out he didn't become emotionally involved with the women he "played" with; they were just friends. Double ick, and I hadn't been anyone's playmate since the fourth grade. What about all that hand-holding, affection, future plan-making? And weren't friends emotionally involved?

And then, as if he knew I needed a new movie twist, he matter-of-factly mentioned that he'd met the Schoolteacher's husband before.

And his girlfriend. "She's married?" I blurted. "Legally . . . although they're just friends now," he replied. Friends, or *friends*? I was confused by what the term even meant anymore. Their crazy setup went beyond the scope of my research. I also saw the irony of my involvement in all this. I had a tendency to gravitate toward noncommittal men, and here I was immersed in a whole bedroomful of noncommittals.

Then a strange thing happened . . . simply by asking questions, I was now being treated as the Engineer's confidante, complete with complaints about the difficulty of keeping up with his open relationship regulations. He kept repeating how this was all new to him, but I wondered. His lack of emotional involvement was clearly something very old. He even admitted his situation "had its perks for the man." Frankly, he was now getting a little too open about his open relationship for me.

The next day he called to inform me that our rendezvous was back on, and did I want to speak with his girlfriend? My heart thumped. At first I said no, but then the ka-ching! of my million-dollar screenplay chimed in. "Sure," I squeaked.

A woman with a warm voice came on the line. "Hi, Katherine." She spoke intelligently and clinically, like schoolteachers (and engineers) are prone to do. She wanted to meet me because "if I can meet a person and know who they are then I feel comfortable with the physical relationship." I learned that she and the Engineer had met in a swingers' club. (New plot point.) She had gone there with her husband and though she knew she wasn't supposed to get emotionally involved with anyone in a swing club, she had. She claimed to be monogamous, but after some background murmuring from the Engineer, she confessed she occasionally slept with her husband, too. And she also put out personal ads, *but* made it clear she was already in love with both her boyfriend and husband. Her definition of monogamy was more fluid than the Pacific Ocean. I made a mental note not to send my future children to her school district.

"Don't you get jealous?" I asked. "Yes," the Schoolteacher admitted, "but between coping with jealousy or the need for variety, I've chosen jealousy." "Don't you want more?" "Yes . . . I do," she said, "I would never have imagined myself in this situation four years ago." The sadness in her voice confused me. "You see, that's why I wanted to meet with you," she went on. "You understand as a woman what it's all about."

We soon discovered that the Engineer had duped her, too, lying that he had told me about their relationship back in Vegas. She apologized for his lie and asked if my feelings were hurt. I was touched by her concern. I then pointed out that he had actually mentioned her a few times but she was always referred to as his friend, not girlfriend. There was dead silence. She put the Engineer back on the phone.

I sensed our meeting was off again, so I finally asked him what I most wanted to know. "Were your affections toward me just an act or did you really feel anything?" He replied it wasn't an act but that he really had to go now. And he clicked off. And so I sat alone with my own mixed feelings. I felt good at having taken a measure of control over the strange situation I found myself in. I felt somewhat enlightened for learning about these exotic open relationship people instead of slamming the door in their faces. I even felt satisfied at having blasted holes in their so-called open model.

But I also felt . . . icky. Although they were the ones who had thrust me into the middle of their soap opera, I had played along and that felt disingenuous. They thought I understood them, when really I didn't. And now I actually felt badly that the Schoolteacher was feeling hurt. Sure, I had wanted some answers and I got them. Why had they left me so unsettled? Maybe because their "open" situation was so distorted by smoke and mirrors, so devoid of any real intimacy, so . . .

Empty.

That's one kind of love, I guess. Not the kind I wanted.

Body Image

♥

Madeleine Beckman

When I met Josef I was on the prowl.

"Join a group," said my therapist. "You might not meet the perfect guy, but you could meet some interesting people."

So, recently "legally separated," I joined Outdoor Bound, a group of New Yorkers, mostly single, mostly women. The ski trip to Vermont consisted of six women and two men, not counting the leader, a man in his early forties who rarely removed his baseball cap.

When we arrived at the ultragingham bed-and-breakfast, we were informed that rain was expected for the entire President's Day weekend. This meant the ski slopes would be turned into rivers of ice and slush. But, we were assured, "there are many things to do in the area."

By this time the women were either vulturing around Josef, a tall, slender bearded man from Germany with a full head of hair, or Steven, about ten years younger, maybe mid-thirties; a playwright, with an effeminate edge. He was flirty with the women. I wasn't convinced.

One day we visited the Maple Syrup Museum. One day we visited the Beeswax Factory. By the third day the rain began to subside. Also by this time, Keiko, a Japanese architect, and I had become pretty inseparable out of desperation for good conversation.

Besides being good-looking, though somewhat severe, Josef was a psychology professor and well read. He was also extremely opinionated.

Steven had a handsome New York Jewish look and was irreverent in that will-not-be-tamed manner of many aspiring playwrights. He had an entitled edge. Vying for "good" dinner seating arrangements at the inn reached vicious proportions.

After dinner most nights, Keiko and I sat around the fire while the others played Scrabble or Monopoly. I leafed through decades-old *Yankee* magazines and drank an almost undrinkable port purchased at the local general store, while she read architectural journals and studied English grammar.

The last day, before we had to get on the van back to New York, the snow and weather conditions turned good; Keiko and I decided to try cross-country skiing. We'd only downhilled before, but the slopes were still closed. We rented skis and were off. Of course, Josef was already in the woods—as if it were springtime—wearing corduroy slacks, a turtleneck, and a hand-knitted sweater, clearly German-made.

Cross-country skiing was exhausting, but fun. Josef was charming and happy to give tips to those who ventured from sitting in front of the fireplace. Afterward, we drank hot chocolates and by 4:00 P.M. were on the van back to New York City. The tour leader, a twice-married, sour, but efficient guy, provided a contact list of everyone and handed these out along with a schedule of upcoming events.

Steven called me and we went out for dinner. He spoke to me about his play-in-progress. I never heard from him again.

A few days later I thought, Seize the moment, and I called Josef. We went to Central Park and walked through the snow. We drank hot ciders on a bench.

We had another date and watched a Buñuel film. And another. We ice-skated at Wollman Rink and drank hot chocolates dispensed from an ancient machine. Again, he wore only corduroy slacks and a Bavarian sweater on his six-foot-two, thin frame.

That night we returned to his apartment on the Upper East Side.

The next morning, after a night of satisfying sex and sleep, I woke, certain I was developing pinkeye. I went to the kitchen to boil water and, attempting to find coffee and cups, found shelves and shelves of vitamins. There were no spices, canned foods, boxes of cereal, glasses, dishes, nada. Did Josef moonlight as a vitamin rep? I opened the fridge and found bottles and jars filled with vitamin elixirs—the type with live cultures that need to be refrigerated.

Then Josef walked in.

"What are you looking for?"

"You have a lot of vitamins," I said.

"I don't like to eat much."

Quickly, I scrolled back in my mind and couldn't recall when he'd eaten anything solid.

He told me about growing up in Germany during the war . . . the story went on about flour rations and margarine.

I had to admit, though sex was good, as my hands stroked his body, I thought, Damn, he's bony. Skeletal actually.

He walked me to the street and hailed a taxi. I sat in the back of the cab as we sped down the FDR, watching the ice on the East River and at New York's skyline. I was happy to be going home.

Once home I made scrambled eggs, bacon, and a side of grits. I put a hot compress on my seeping eye and felt a little sad.

Josef had done nothing terrible. But I loved to eat and cook and go out to restaurants. I wrote articles about food and culture. There was a huge part of me I'd need to deny being with Josef and I knew the ending.

"You have to have your nonnegotiables," my therapist had said more than once.

Yes, there was kindness, and sense of humor, intellect, sex, and values. But there were also those things that brought me joy. Would I be able to be with someone who found no pleasure in eating? Sharing food? Eating what I cooked? Baked?

No. But I did learn how to cross-country ski.

A Cautionary Tale

♥

Liz Dubelman

Never fall in love on vacation. The dictionary says the definition of vacation is: period of rest, leisure, recreation, or travel, esp. away from one's regular occupation. Strike *occupation* and read *life*. I was living in New York when I met this man (we'll call him the Antichrist) while on vacation. Everyone, even the Antichrist, is great on vacation, especially on a holiday at Vista Clare, a New Age spa in the middle of the New Mexican desert. The Antichrist was, at least in this incarnation, a recently divorced father of three from Los Angeles. Ten days later the vacation was over and I couldn't live without this man.

I know this would be a good place to tell you all why I thought this man so captivating, lest you think of me as defective in some way, but I don't remember much. Chalk it up to Post-Break-Up Syndrome, or PUS. (We're working on securing the URL www.pus.com.) PUS is the mind's way of protecting us from proving to ourselves that we're stupid. It's somewhere between a repressed memory (unconscious) and a selected memory (conscious). I know there was sex involved. And, in my defense, my lapse in judgment sent me straight into analysis.

Anyway, I followed the Antichrist to Los Angeles and before too long I felt like this was not my beautiful life. I'd say it broke down like this: two weeks of naïve bliss, two weeks of this is weird, two weeks of how do I convince him we need fixing.

There were many, many warning signs. I should have known my first day in town. I had rented a small apartment over a very expensive celebrity-ridden restaurant at the beach. The Antichrist had arrived ten hours late to help me unpack. Something had come up with the children. He seemed upset. I was a wreck by the time he got there, but I didn't want to frighten him away. After all, he was the only person I knew in L.A. He suggested we go out to dinner at the restaurant downstairs. We had no reservation but the Antichrist cajoled, wheedled, and bullied his way in. I should have known then, but I actually saw that as charming. It was like being on the inside of a con. It seemed like safer danger.

The dinner was lovely. The table was set with this one-of-a-kind hand-painted tableware. I innocently commented on how exquisite everything was. I excused myself to the ladies' room while he paid the check. He met me outside by the elevator. He seemed flushed. When we got upstairs he presented me with two coffee cups from the tableware collection downstairs. He said he paid for them but the cups still had coffee residue inside.

Safer danger was beginning to turn into dangerous danger. The third week into my L.A. mistake I realized I was paying for everything. He never had any cash or even a credit card on him, yet he showered me with expensive gifts. I was confused and creeped out. He became more and more distant. I suggested couples' therapy. He said I was just like his ex-wife. Yikes. Is there anything worse to tell a girlfriend?

One day we were alone together. He was surfing the Net and I was drinking coffee from my hand-painted, one-of-a-kind coffee cup from the restaurant downstairs and reading my horoscope. My astrological forecast read: No matter how you try to ignore dysfunctional tendency, it's not going away. Could everyone in my sun sign be going through the same thing at the same time? The phone rang. The Antichrist answered and, although he said nothing, he was shaken. The phone rang again and the Antichrist opened the front door and left, with the rings chiming behind him. I answered.

"I know what he did," a man said. "Get him some help or I'm calling the police."

What did this man know? What was the Antichrist doing? Okay, "get him some help." There you go. Something to do. I can always find solace in doing. I paged through the phone book. What was I looking for? Nothing under "Help." To a nice Jewish girl "help" means therapy. At least I felt that that was a safe bet for help. I found a mental health clinic and made an appointment for Monday at noon.

Monday at eleven I informed the Antichrist of the appointment, and that I would, of course, pay for it. To my surprise he was willing to go, which only infused my optimism. The therapist, a man we'll call Dr. Moses, listened and was especially curious about the phone call and my unflappable dedication to this doomed relationship. The Antichrist said nothing. Eventually, Dr. Moses asked me to leave the room so he could talk to the Antichrist in private.

Later that night I received *the phone call*. The Dr. Moses call.

"I'm glad you answered," Dr. Moses said. "I've never done this before. This situation you're in . . . um, you need to leave."

"Excuse me?" I said. "I don't understand."

"You and your boyfriend. It's not going to work out. You need to leave him. He's um . . ."

"What? Gay?" I don't know why I said that. It just seemed like something we couldn't get over.

"No, he's . . . he's a kleptomaniac. I hope you find what you're looking for, but this is not it."

Well. You don't have to hit me over the head.

I Knew It Was Over...

♥

Patricia Marx

I knew it was over when he dumped me.

The Authors

♡

MADELEINE BECKMAN is the author of *Dead Boyfriends,* a poetry collection; her poetry, fiction, and articles have been published nationally and internationally. She is the recipient of awards and grants, including a Hemingway Award and the Heinrich Böll Foundation grant (IE).

FRANCESCA LIA BLOCK is the award-winning author of many novels and stories, including the bestselling Weetzie Bat series. She lives in Los Angeles with her children.

ZOE BRAVERMAN is currently a multicampus University of California student. She dabbles in writing of all kinds, most recently screenwriting. She is chasing her dreams in the city where they allegedly come true, Los Angeles, and is happily involved with someone who does like her in "that way."

BONNIE BRUCKHEIMER is known for producing such films as *Beaches* and *Divine Secrets of the Ya-Ya Sisterhood,* but is most proud of her role as mother of Keith Martell (age twenty-one) and Miranda Martell (age sixteen).

MARYEDITH BURRELL has starred in five TV series, written and/or produced fourteen screenplays, and also directs for the stage. She recently got married and inherited a teenage daughter. What was she thinking?

DEBBIE CAVANAUGH has published two novels, *Love Thy Neighbor* and *Where There's a Will.* She has also published several children's books and many articles.

LAURA CELLA is a native New Yorker with a master's degree in English from New York University who teaches poetry and fiction to high school juniors and seniors.

KERRI CESENE is a painter who lives in the Hudson River Valley in New York with her husband and two children.

CINDY CHUPACK was a writer and executive producer of HBO's *Sex and the City* and is the author of *The Between Boyfriends Book: A Collection of Cautiously Hopeful Essays* (www.betweenboyfriends.com).

AIMEE CIRUCCI is a Philadelphia-area writer who enjoys finding the humorous side of family, foibles, and failed relationships. She can be reached at www.cirucci.com and she still doesn't like video games.

DARBY CLARK is a serial entrepreneur who currently runs a management and marketing firm in Manhattan. For fun she blogs on www.musewithme.net and continues her lifelong study of dance and movement.

KATE COE has been producing nonfiction television since the mid-eighties. Most recently she has collaborated with the filmmakers Yareli Arizmendi, Sergio Arau, Burt Kearns, Ken Bowser, Larry Charles, and Bill Maher as an archival footage consultant and expert in clearance, licensing, and fair use. She also writes frequently on media for *LA Weekly, Fast Company, Grist,* and other publications.

MELINDA CULEA was an actress for twenty-five years. She is now working on her first novel. She lives in California with her husband and two children.

BARBARA DAVILMAN writes and produces reality television and writes humor books with her husband, Ellis Weiner. They live in Los Angeles with their dogs Peaches and Jaxon and their foster dog, Chester.

JUDITH DEWEY received her M.F.A. from Cornell University and has worked as an actress and writer on stage, TV, and in film. She has been happily married for more than twenty-five years to a man without a unibrow, and has raised two brilliantly talented children.

SARAH DOWNIE is an attorney. She lives in Manhattan. She enjoys playing with her cat, boxing, and avoiding difficult conversations.

LIZ DUBELMAN (with her partner, Paca Thomas) owns VidLit Productions (www.vidlit.com). She lives in Los Angeles with her husband, Paul Slansky, and their daughter, Grace. What she's thinking can usually be found in her Facebook status updates.

TINA DUPUY is a stand-up comedian who failed into journalism. She currently subsidizes both by blogging. She lives in Los Angeles with her husband and her dog of indiscernible breed.

MARY FEUER writes for the TV show *Dante's Cove* and created the Web series *With the Angels*. Her fiction has been published in *Writer's Digest* and *Southern Indiana Review*.

CARRIE FISHER is a writer and actress who frequently finds herself wondering, What was I thinking?

GERALYN FLOOD is a transplanted New Yorker who lives (and drives!) in Los Angeles. She is a casting director who has worked on film and television.

AMY FRIEDMAN writes the syndicated column *Tell Me a Story,* which has spawned award-winning audiobooks. She has published two memoirs and lives and teaches in Los Angeles.

MICHELE GENDELMAN is an author *(What the Other Mothers Know)* and a screen and television writer. She lives in Los Angeles with her wonderful second husband, writer and producer Andy Guerdat.

BETTY GOLDSTEIN started writing three years ago. She loves writing down moments from her life, and tending to her husband and son.

COURTENAY HAMEISTER is a freelance writer and host of *Live Wire!* on Oregon public broadcasting. She is shocked to be in this anthology, as her taste in men is usually just absolutely fucking spot-on.

WENDY HAMMERS on the page: tousmesregimes.com (Marabout Press). On the tube: *Curb Your Enthusiasm, The Sopranos, The Late Late Show with Craig Ferguson.* On the stage: *You've Got Meal.* Also visit www.wendyhammers.com.

CLAUDIA HANDLER is a New Yorker who currently lives in L.A. She has written songs and fiction, but is best known for her poetry. She is the author of *Going Under.*

NICOLE HOLLANDER is the creator of the nationally syndicated cartoon strip *Sylvia.* Her new book is *Tales of Graceful Aging from the Planet Denial,* published by Broadway Books.

MONICA JOHNSON is a television and screen writer who cowrote the films *Real Life, Modern Romance, Lost in America, Mother, The Scout, Jekyll and Hyde Together Again, Americathon,* and *The Muse.* She also wrote on and/or produced *Laverne and Shirley, It's Garry Shandling's Show,* and many other TV shows. She just finished her first novel, *The Penny Saver.* She currently lives in the desert with her imaginary friends.

DEBORAH RACHEL KAGAN is a regular on the Los Angeles spoken word scene. *Hello, Pussy,* her collection of short stories, will be published in 2009. She lusts for the perfect tea latte.

DORIT SIMONE K. F. is a writer, producer, and performing artist. She graduated from N.Y.U. with honors and is currently pursuing her career in Los Angeles.

MAIRA KALMAN (author, illustrator, and ex-girlfriend of idiot boyfriend) lives and works in New York City.

MARY-MARGARET MARTINEZ is a writer, filmmaker, and undiscovered genius living in quiet solitude in the tiny hamlet of Los Angeles, California. She is currently at work on a midlife crisis.

PATRICIA MARX is a staff writer for *The New Yorker.* Her last novel was *Him Her Him Again The End of Him.* She is a former party event planner for the CIA.

KERRY MONAGHAN is a writer and editor. She shares her time between Brooklyn and Crete, Greece, where she is writing her first novel.

MARYJANE MORRISON writes fiction, episodic television, and features, including the biopic *Howard Hughes: His Women and His Movies.* She lives and works in Venice, California.

LISA NAPOLI is a journalist who lives in Los Angeles and has, most recently, worked for the public radio show *Marketplace.* Her book about Bhutan, *Three Good Things: What I Learned in the Happiest Place on Earth,* will be published by Crown in 2010.

SARA NEWBERRY, a Texas native, lives in Brooklyn with her sweet dog and not-so-sweet cat. She remains hopeful.

RACHAEL PARENTA is a writer and comedian living in Brooklyn. She appeared on *The Richard Simmons Show* in 1983.

LYNN SNOWDEN PICKET's work can be seen in *Vogue, Self,* and *O* magazines, as well as many other publications. She is the author of *Nine Lives: From Stripper to Schoolteacher* and *Looking for a Fight,* a memoir.

MIMI POND is a writer and cartoonist whose work currently appears regularly in the *Los Angeles Times.* She lives in Los Angeles.

KARA POST-KENNEDY is a screenwriter who has written more than a dozen scripts, many on commission. Some of these have come dangerously close to being entered in festivals or even produced! She is a happily married mother of a wonderful son, whom she is now busy teaching how to flush the toilet.

RACHEL RESNICK is the author of the memoir *Love Junkie* (Bloomsbury). She lives in Los Angeles and travels around the world running luxury writing retreats with the internationally acclaimed program Writers On Fire (www.writersonfire.com).

JEANNE ROMANO is single and, according to her mother, incapable of changing that status. After twenty-five years of living in Hollywood, being a writer and producer for network television, Jeanne made the big move to Seattle, which is, as we all know, the Northwest hub for nothing that relates to her previous life—but hey, her hair and skin look great!

KATHERINE RUPPE is a screenwriter in Venice, California. She recently married the man of her dreams, a rock 'n' roll musician who thankfully brought only himself and a whole lotta love to the relationship.

COURTNEY S. could be any Courtney S. It is a common name. It is not necessarily the Courtney S. you know, even if it does sound just like her. If her in-laws are reading this, no, it is not the sweet girl you let your son marry.

HILARY SCHWARTZ is a stand-up comedian and member of the comedic music act, the Manson Family Singers. Originally from Washington, D.C., she now lives in New York City.

HANNAH ROSE SHAFFER lives in western Massachusetts with her scruffy white dog and a few scruffy boys. She is currently studying human sexuality, video art, and creative writing at Hampshire College.

JANICE SHAPIRO and JESSICA WOLK-STANLEY live in New York and Seattle. They are working on a comic book, *Love Is Dumb*, which is going to be really good and which everyone will like a lot.

PENNY STALLINGS is the author of several books on popular culture including *Flesh and Fantasy* and *Rock 'n' Roll Confidential*. She has been an essayist for *The NewsHour* on PBS and the cocreator of the Nickelodeon sitcom, *Hi Honey, I'm Home*.

RHONDA TALBOT is a film executive who moonlights as a writer. Her first novel, *A Halfway Decent Girl*, was published in 2002. She also writes for film and television.

KATHERINE TOMLINSON still believes true love is possible, although she no longer believes in Santa Claus or the Tooth Fairy. She lives in Los Angeles.

AMY TURNER was a staff writer on *Studio 60* and her first book, *He Typed, She Typed*, was published in 2008 by Full Court Press. Turner is a product of Orange County.

LAURIE WINER is thrilled to be back on Broadway, where previously she headlined in *WHAT TH—?* with Garth Barth and Sally the Eight-Foot Woman. Previous credits include Shmendrik in *Antony and Cleopatra*, Cleopatra in *The Johnny Unitas Story*, Third Noblewoman in *Auntie! (The William Finn Musical of Sophocles's Antigone, by Fucking Sophocles, Okay?)*, Momma Tokyo Rose in *Hey Amelican G.I. Joe, Everything Coming Up Hershey Bar You Sullendah*, and Eliza Donothing in *True Waste*.

JAN WORTHINGTON lived for fifteen years in Los Angeles, where she wrote more than thirty movies for television. She now lives on Cape Cod, where she is working on a memoir.

AMY WRUBLE is a television producer and writer in Los Angeles whose search for love has not yet yielded a husband but has provided endless opportunities for storytelling.